Testimonials

"Jacqui DeLorenzo's indomitable spirit shines throughout this book. This isn't so much a story of survival as it is of transcendence over all manner of difficult circumstances, one day at a time. Jacqui's honest portrayal of her very human struggles and ultimate triumphs will remind others that there is always the choice between being a victim and being a conqueror. Anyone who reads this book will learn that Jacqui is the ultimate conqueror. Her story of creating a life worth living in the face of considerable adversity will undoubtedly inspire many readers to become conquerors as well."
Carolyn Bailey, MA, LMHC

"This is a memoir written straight from the heart of a woman whose determination to heal and thrive is incomparable. Jacqui never falters in her faith despite the many profound challenges she faces. Her story is one that graces the reader with the enduring resilience of her spirit."
Judy E. Gould, MS, LMHC

"Jacqui DeLorenzo fearlessly and eloquently provides us with a detailed account of her traumas and triumphs. *A Thread of Hope* is an inspirational must-read for anyone who is a survivor of childhood traumas and is struggling to regain inner peace and hope."
Jennifer McCarthy, MEd, MS, LMHC

A Thread of Hope

Sheldon,
  may the angels
always carry you on
their wings.
  Always hang on to
that Thread of Hope.
  God Bless !

Jacqui

A Thread of Hope

✦

A Woman's Spiritual Journey of Faith from Trauma to Triumph

Jacqui DeLorenzo, MS, LMHC

iUniverse, Inc.
New York Lincoln Shanghai

A Thread of Hope
A Woman's Spiritual Journey of Faith from Trauma to Triumph

iUniverse books may be ordered through booksellers or by contacting:

iUniverse
2021 Pine Lake Road, Suite 100
Lincoln, NE 68512
www.iuniverse.com
1-800-Authors (1-800-288-4677)

Because of the dynamic nature of the Internet, any Web addresses or links contained in this book may have changed since publication and may no longer be valid.

Many of the names in this book have been changed. My intent in writing this book is not to hurt, harm, or cause pain to anyone; on the contrary, my intent is to give hope and help others overcome obstacles in their lives despite the adversities they have faced.

First Paperback Edition

ISBN: 978-0-595-44766-4 (pbk)
ISBN: 978-0-595-68966-8 (cloth)
ISBN: 978-0-595-89085-9 (ebk)

Printed in the United States of America

To Rick Voit, PhD
He helped me discover who I am.

If our eyes could not see, how beautiful we would see the world through our hearts.
Jacqui DeLorenzo, MS, Licensed Mental Health Counselor

Contents

Acknowledgments

My Family

Thanks to my mom, Anita, who literally saved my life—I knew she always loved me and continues to do so with all her being. To my sister, Jeanne: together we survived the fears, the sorrows, and the pains of our childhood. And to my sister, Debbie: I could always count on her, no matter what.

In Loving Memory

In loving memory of my baby sister, Mary, who I never got to know but who is with me in spirit. In loving memory of my dear little brother, Johnny, whom I loved with all my heart. I thank him for the courage and strength he gave to me throughout my life, especially during my bout with cancer. My grandmother, Lea, who I loved with all my heart and who loved me equally. She was indeed the best of the best. In loving memory of my cousin, Tony, who helped me make memorable childhood memories. My beloved friends Marguerite and Doris, who I miss very much but who remain in my heart.

My Friends

Anne: who has given me her warmth, love, and friendship and is indeed my earth angel., Barbara: a friend and co-worker who has been a travel companion and a terrific listener., Carolyn: a friend with whom I shared my trials and tribulations along with my joys, as she did with me., Cathy: a dear friend who helped me promote this book., Cindy: a dear friend who has always given me much support., Donna: a dear friend who I see regularly to share our morning coffee and friendship., Donna: a good friend who I met through my sister Jeanne., Ellyn: my friend who has shown me sincere friendship., Jennifer (BB): a friend to whom I am bonded with a special soul connection., Joan: my friend who helped me immensely by organizing my journals so I could begin my journey to write this book., Joyce: a long-time friend and former co-worker helped me make a memorable college "event," for which we worked so many years together., Judy: my friend and supervisory guide in obtaining my LMHC license., Judy: a dear friend who I met through the North Shore chapter of St. Jude., Kathy: a friend with whom I share a deep friendship that has kept us connected throughout the years.. Kerry: a dear friend who worked with me to help our mutually beloved friend, Marguerite., Larry: a true blue, dedicated, family friend., Linda: a long-time dear friend with whom I share a special connection., Louise: a dear friend who shared with me friendship, love, and memorable vacations., Lynne: a dear college friend with whom I've continued to share many fun times., Marilyn: my long-time, dedicated, true blue friend., Nancy: a friend with whom I have shared much fun and many exciting times., Sandy: a true friend I can always count on, and who is indeed selfless., Susan G: a dear NSCC friend who has always supported me with kindness, concern, and friendship., Terri: a long-time dear friend who is caring and kind., Tina: my special childhood friend, who stuck by me through the worst years of my life, and who helped me suffer through my own private hell, as I tried to help her survive her own.

And to all my friends never to be forgotten: Ali, Anne P., Barbara E., Barbara K., Betty (Maria B), Carol, Cathy B., Coral, Diane, Dominic, Donna, Dylanie, Elaine O., Irene, Jean K., Joanne H., Julie, Kathy, Laura, Lil, Marianne, Maria G., Marie A., Martine, Mary, Mel, Pam G., Susan D., Susan W.S., Sally Z., and Tricia.

In Thanksgiving

I want to thank all my friends who gave me their gifts of friendship, love, understanding, and patience. I love you all and thank you from the deepest part of my heart.

Thank you to the doctors that saved my life. Thank you to my surgeon and primary care physician, Dr. McGilvrary. Thank you to my oncologists, Dr. J. Lokich and Dr. Suit. Thank you to all the nurses and staff who helped me through this ordeal.

Thank you: God, Holy Spirit, Sacred Heart of Jesus, Mary Mother of God, St. Jude, St. Theresa, St. Anthony, and St. Joseph.

Special thanks to all the angels above who continue to protect and guide me on my journeys through life.

In Gratitude & Special Thanks

In Gratitude
North Shore Community College

Massachusetts General Hospital
Dana Farber Cancer Institute

My Goal Group Pals:
    Carolyn, Jennifer, Lori, Kirsten, Terri, Tina, Vaughn

Special Thanks

To Kathy Sands-Boehmer, for helping me with her amazing skills, Therese (Terri) Kay, for her great photography tkayphotography@verizon.net, Cathy Dunne, Baystate Professional Book Services, Inc. for helping in the promotion of this book. www.baystatebooks.com, and. Anne Tabet, for her helping me complete a dream I've held in my heart Jessie Inz, LICSW.

Special thoughts and prayers

Cheryl Richardson, who inspired me to keep journeying.
Warm thoughts to Oprah Winfrey, who I have always admired and loved.
James Van Praagh, a true Ghost Whisperer
David Pelzer, a man who I admire for his courage and strength

Preface

"I am," I cried, "I am," said I, and I am lost, and I can't even say why. Leaving me lonely still.

I could feel the pain of these words by Neil Diamond deep inside my soul. The pain would not let me go. It hung on tight and drove me to the depths of depression. I hurt so badly. My only friend was the radio, and it truly was my friend. Why did I hurt and why couldn't anyone see—and, even more importantly, why didn't they care?

When I started to think about what I was going to name my book I thought about naming it after another song on the radio. It told a story about a person's painful childhood and how unloved he had felt, only to discover that he had to love himself first before he could feel loved by anyone else. I found out later in life that I had to learn to love myself before anyone else could love me.

Once I began writing this book I was often asked why I chose to expose so much of my life to a public readership. First of all, I am not ashamed of my life but proud of my accomplishments. I couldn't always say this because I didn't always feel this way, but now I want to help people who have been through similar experiences to know they are not alone. There is light at the end of that dark tunnel and this time it's not the train but rather a bright light full of a great future of hopes, plans, and dreams that actually become reality.

Deep within one's soul is always a thread of hope, even if you can barely feel it. I want you to hang onto that thread and watch it grow into a thick rope that is impossible to fray. Life can be extremely cruel, but if you can learn from its harsh realities then you can build a strong character that one might think is beyond his or her reach. I came to a point in my life when the realities were too painful and I didn't want to exist anymore, but within my desperation I found this thread of hope. I decided to hang onto it, and you can, too.

Growing up in the sixties was tough. Prejudices were strong. As a child I didn't know who I was, but I grew up believing I was less than everyone else because my peers constantly made me feel inferior. My once outgoing personality shrunk and shriveled like a grape that had been left out in the sun. I felt like a nobody.

My heart goes out to all of you who have experienced and endured unbearable pain, bullying, discrimination, and adversity, and my hope is that this book will give you the courage to march on with that thread of hope. Life has so much to offer and it is not beyond your reach. Don't give up—you'll be glad you didn't!

I would like to extend to anyone reading this book to feel free to visit my website at http://threadofhope.wordpress.com and to contact me at my e-mail address: Jacquiannd@yahoo.com. God bless!

Introduction

I come from a family of five children. I am the second oldest. My sister Jeanne was born first, and my sister Debbie was born five years after me. My baby sister Mary was born fourth in the family but died when she was only three days old, from an infection she got while in the nursery at the hospital. My brother Johnny was born ten years after me. He was the fifth and final child. He died of leukemia at the age of thirteen.

Debbie, Jacqui + Jeanne

Our family seemed to be picture-perfect, but things aren't always as they appear. My father chose to leave our "happy" home and because of this I felt traumatized and my life's path was forever changed. My family became very structured after my father left. My mom was firm with us, and we knew she meant what she said. None of us wanted to make her angry.

I was close to my older sister growing up, probably because we bonded through the tough times when the vicious fights happened between my parents. Jeanne and I were very close in age and we shared secrets, and comforted each other. We shared a room and we protected each other. We were only twenty-three months apart but we felt even closer and we were always there for each other. But really, we were quite individual. I looked up to her and often wished I were like her. I felt empty and alone and she seemed to have it all. I felt like I was always searching for some kind of an elusive butterfly, but I was never able to catch it.

My younger sister Debbie and I got along well. I was her big sister, after all. I'd listen to her and help her, and we were friends, too. She was treated differently than my sister Jeanne and me. I often said later as the years went by that she grew up in a "different house." My mom had a whole other set of rules for Debbie. She let up on her a bit, allowing her far more freedoms than Jeanne and I were given. Maybe by the time Debbie came around, times had changed again, and so had my mom—somewhat, anyway.

I had a special relationship with my brother, Johnny. I considered him my baby. I helped my mom with him. I fed him, changed him, and played games with him. As he grew older, we grew even closer. He would look up to me for guidance and security. We went for long rides and talked the whole time. I was devastated when he was diagnosed with leukemia. I thought it was so unfair that a twelve-year-old would be stricken with such a deadly disease, especially when that twelve-year-old was my brother. I nurtured him through his cancer (Chapter 13 is dedicated to him), but little did I realize that I would draw on that strength when I battled my own cancer (a topic in Chapter 16). I loved him. Cancer took his life nine months after he was diagnosed. I couldn't even cry at his wake. I guess I was all cried out from my childhood and would not let his dying hurt me. I built a wall around me then, a wall that was crumbling every day, a little at a time, eroding the inner depths of my being.

But, still, we were always a close-knit family. We had to be; we had to stick together. We only had each other to depend on and love. We were all fighting our own personal heartaches, but as a family we decided that it was important to be there for one another. One of our ways of accomplishing this is that we all ate supper together every night. There were times when we didn't say much and times when we did, but the important thing was that we were together as a family. We may not have had lobster and steak, but my mother always made sure we ate well and our bellies were full. We never went to bed hungry.

We each had our designated chores. We all chipped in to help keep house. I was in charge of dusting. My mom had beautiful Hummels. They were strategically placed along a half-wall on many horizontal and vertical shelves, and dusting them was not an easy task. My next chore was vacuuming. We had wall-to-wall rugs and tile floors. I also folded the laundry, stacked and un-stacked the dishwasher, and put the groceries in their proper places. I had to make sure that the green beans were together and the carrots were together, et cetera. I even had them in alphabetical order so they could be easily found. I was a little obsessive compulsive wouldn't you say? I got upset if someone disrupted my strategically placed vegetables. Every Saturday, I had to do my chores before I could do anything else. My mom was extremely strict and there was no negotiating.

We had to obey the rules. My mother was relentless. I felt she was overly strict but I was just a kid trying to survive. One time my sister dilly-dallied and consequently did not have time to make her bed and meet the school bus. My mother insisted that my sister make her bed. She missed the bus. This was the last time she didn't leave enough time to make her bed. I remember being punished for not being home before the lights went on along our street. She had this cowbell that she would cling-clang. If we were in ears' reach we were lucky, because we had five extra minutes to get home. I think my mom felt she had to take control to keep herself from feeling like she had lost it.

Mom + Dad in happier times

After my dad left our home, my mom became very depressed. She was left alone with four small children, hardly any money, and much uncertainty of what was to become of our family. She had no one to turn to, but she had all the responsibility and was overwhelmed by it. Unlike my sisters, I felt responsible for making things better for our family, and especially for my mom. I didn't have many resources, but I knew that my mother's heart was broken and I wanted to mend it. I wanted to see her smile again. I wanted my family to be happy. I was out to save my mom and my family, but who was going to save me?

I was hated and continually bullied at school by mean, cruel-spirited kids. Looking back, I suppose I must have seemed like an easy target. I was someone they could hurt to make themselves feel better and feel powerful. I was hurting from my home life and couldn't get the comfort I needed at school, especially when kids there chose me to be their dartboard. I wanted to be protected from their wrath. I wanted a place to feel safe. I wanted someone to believe me. I needed validation and someone to take away the enormous pain that I endured every day of my life.

I went around unnoticed at home, not getting what I needed most. My mom was so wrapped up in her own pain that she failed to see my pain. Her tears that filled her entire being blinded her, and she couldn't see me. But I needed her. My siblings were not tormented the way I was at school. I believed that I was a freak, different from all of them, and that it was very noticeable. I was told how ugly and fat I was, and how I looked like a monkey. I was continually taunted with racial slurs that frightened me. Their nastiness left an indelible mark on how I felt about my skin color. I was told in such a demeaning and cruel way that I grew to believe that to have a dark complexion meant I was unworthy and less than. Their torture stayed with me for years and the echoes of their voices have rung clearly in my head throughout my life.

My siblings didn't demand the attention I so craved, perhaps because they weren't being treated as I was. I remember several times walking up the driveway to the bus stop and being physically sick from nerves. I knew what was in store for me from the moment I got on the school bus to the moment I got off the school bus. I couldn't wait to grow up and not have to go to school. Each weekend as Sunday evening came around, I got a sick feeling in my stomach and knew in my heart I was in for another horrible week. To me, school meant being harassed and bullied with no one to save me. The nuns looked the other way when the kids were so cruel. They had their own agenda.

I realize now how insecure those kids were, as most kids are at that age. I understand that it made them feel powerful to make someone else feel so sad and badly about themselves. I prayed and prayed to die, and prayed that if I couldn't die, Jesus would help me through the day. I prayed it would end. I prayed and never lost faith. I hung onto a thread, a thread of hope. The cruel treatment didn't end, though; instead it got worse.

I remember being alone in my room one afternoon after school. I had taken a bottle of aspirin from the medicine cabinet and went to my room and closed the door. I thought about my life and how miserable I was and contemplated taking the whole bottle of aspirin. I couldn't stand the pain any longer. I so very much wanted to die. I felt no one cared except my mom, but she couldn't help me; I didn't feel she truly believed me when I told her what I was experiencing. In the next room I heard my mom sobbing so loudly that I could hear her cries through the closed door of my bedroom. I remember thinking that it would hurt her so badly if I accomplished the deed I intended. I knew deep in my heart that she loved me; that she was the *only* one who loved me. She needed me, and I needed to protect her. I had to make it my life's goal to make her happy, and then, only then, maybe I would be happy, too.

In those bad times, I really didn't feel I was good at anything. I felt like shit. It was difficult for me to live day-to-day. While my sister Jeanne was angry with my mother for my father leaving, I blamed the other woman for stealing my daddy. I wanted my daddy; he was mine and I loved him. We had him first, and it wasn't fair that someone could come along and snatch him like a thief. This made me beyond sad. I wondered why the other woman couldn't find someone else. *Why? Why? Why?* Did she know the pain we were all feeling? Did she care? Thoughts like these constantly rang in my head. The pain grew deeper and stronger.

I was the peacemaker. I believed getting angry would result in someone leaving. So I stuffed my anger deep within me, leaving me depressed, empty, and alone. I'd decided that my job was to protect my mom, but that meant not having any kind of a child's life myself. I stayed home to "take care" of Mom. I remember feeling so upset with my life then that I went to my room after school and pulled the hair out of my head. I ended up with little bald spots that I attempted to cover up so that no one would notice. In a strange way, it actually felt good to feel the physical pain that seemed to match my mental anguish. It took the place of the deep pain in my heart and soul at least for the moment. I was embarrassed at myself for doing this, and I knew it was not normal, but I couldn't help myself; nor at that point did I want to try. No one ever caught on to what I was doing, and this habit continued for some time. Later on I replaced it with another self-destructive activity.

I personally never knew who I was as a child. I developed my own inner world, a place where I could go where no one else was allowed. A place where no one could hurt me where I drowned in the music that cried with me. I could dream and not be afraid it would be taken away from me. Music became my life; I loved country western music. I sang along with the music and knew every heart-wrenching word. Each singer's story was my own. Finally, I could feel that someone understood because I could hear that each singer, too, felt the pain.

Neil Diamond was my favorite pop artist. He spoke volumes in his words of loneliness and being alone. He cried and he wanted to be loved and needed. "For I am a man who doesn't swear, but I never cared for the sound of being alone, "I am, I said," he crooned. Now, I was not alone and someone out there felt it too. I listened to all types of music. I loved country, soft rock, and easy music. I loved listening to Neil Diamond and Elton John or anyone who sang out to me morning, noon, and night. I'd listen in the car, in my house, and in the privacy of my own room. I could cry until my eyes swelled so that they were nearly closed shut. There was no stopping. I would cry forever. I wanted to stop, but I needed a reason to stop. Sometimes I thought that maybe I would stop crying, but that thought flew very quickly out of my head. I wanted the pain to stop. I wanted to be happy like everyone else seemed to be. But when I listened to music, I hung onto a thread of hope, even if it was just a very thin thread.

My parent's breakup, my sister's death, my brother's catastrophic illness, my own personal trials with cancer and an eating disorder, my tortuous childhood years, and the life we as a family endured held more than enough pain for a lifetime. Today, as I look back, I see that our family learned to survive the adverse conditions of daily pain by just trying to make it through the day. However, with each other's help, we grew stronger as individuals, able to find our own identities. It took much longer for me to find mine, but the strong foundation of who I was emerged with a lot of help. Before this, my self-esteem had so diminished that it was as though I sat in an open field, a sparrow with a broken wing—unable to fly. The predators were there to attack me, and they did, using every opportunity.

For anyone who has been tormented and bullied and has suffered prejudice, this book will touch your heart and hit a nerve. You will not feel alone because you are not alone. I believe you when you say it is really as bad as you say it is. I believe you when you say you are not exaggerating. I believe you, because it happened to me, and I know it happens all the time.

My goal in life was to prove to everyone that I wasn't really like what I thought they saw. I wanted to prove that I was really okay. For a long time, the problem with wanting to accomplish this enormous task was that I didn't believe it myself. I grew up feeling depressed and alone, feeling that I would never belong in a community. I always felt different than everybody else, and I thought everyone else knew this. I *knew* I was different. I didn't know why, and I couldn't understand any of it. What I learned since then is that "there is no future in the past." Blame is not mine to own, but responsibility for what happens to me and how I handle the struggles, ups and downs, pleasures, and displeasures is indeed my own.

This is my story.

me at six years of age in my backyard

1

Early Years

Looking back on my childhood I vividly remember very few things before my third birthday. I lived in Salem, Massachusetts, with my mom, dad, and my sister Jeanne. We lived on the second floor of my grandmother's house. My grandmother was brought up in a French speaking home, as an adult she taught herself English. My grandfather born in Canada, grew up in a French spoken home therefore, my grandparents raised their family speaking only French. My mother took classes to learn the English language. I remember when I got angry with my mom I would run away from home. Running away from home simply meant going down the back steps to my grandmother's door, where she would welcome me with open arms. She would rock me and sing French songs, hoping that I would learn her language. I did want to learn the language to please her. My mom, although she could speak and understand French fluently, did not speak French to us in our home. I believe she used it as a code to keep us from knowing what she was talking about when she talked with my grandmother. She never had to spell out words, which some people do with young children who can't spell yet; instead she simply said them in French, unless she was with my dad. My dad didn't understand French. Growing up I knew very little about my Italian decent due to my father's absence at a very young age. He was of Italian descent, but my mom didn't know Italian, so they spoke English together and spelled words when they needed to so their children couldn't understand them. I was a happy child and full of confidence, before I started school. I loved to sing and act and make people laugh. I remember entertaining my dad's family by singing and dancing to the Mexican hat dance. I would pass around a straw hat to get coins for my piggy bank. I was loved and I knew it. The strong foundation blocks that were being built then would help me later on in my journey to survive the harsh realities of life.

In 1954 our family moved to a town about ten miles away. This was a sad time for my mom and grandmother. Although it was only ten miles away, it might as well been fifty. My grandmother didn't drive, and my mom was too busy with a new baby, my sister, and me to visit with her. It was a big adjustment. No longer could I run away from home to spend time with my dear grandmother. The new town was rural in those days, and we lived four miles from town, which was a long way and certainly not feasible for walking when you were only five years old.

Our new home was beautiful, but we all missed my grandmother terribly. She was the best. We could call her but it wasn't like seeing her. At the beginning, she would sometimes visit us and sleep over. However, my grandfather never wanted to stay at our home. He loved his home, and coming to stay with us meant that my grandmother would have to leave him during those times. This was not an easy adjustment for him. She would make him meals in advance so he wouldn't starve. He was not too fond of this arrangement so it was lucky for him that my grandmother rarely stayed with us.

My grandmother did stay with us for a longer period after my mom had my brother John. My mom was very sick and suffered from post-partum depression. My grandmother saved our family then by helping my mom back on her feet. She was truly our Earth Angel.

Lucky for me I met my life-long friend Tina. I was not used to being so far away from other houses, stores, a big park, and the ocean yet, but Tina lived across the street from our house. I also lived next door to my cousin, Tony. We were all about the same age, and we used to meet each other between our houses to play together and have picnics and grape soda. We had a swing set and it had a great slide. We played with our dogs and had a great time just being kids. Tony was a great cousin and pal. We still saw each other periodically, until he passed away on June 9, 2006. Tina and I remain very close friends.

My summers back then consisted of going to the beach on the Gloucester shore; playing jump rope, hop scotch, and red light; having cookouts; riding my bike, which I was never really good at; playing with Tina and Tony; and enjoying the warmth of the summer sun that I so loved. I never was a winter person. I hated the cold and never wanted to venture out into it. My mom would bundle me up and send me out for fresh air. I didn't like sledding or ice-skating because it was always so cold. I just couldn't warm up, and it was never long before I headed back inside to go to the bathroom. I think being cold just set off my bladder. My mom eventually got tired of dressing and undressing me for such short periods of time. I was happy to stay in and play with my toys, color in my coloring book, and make cards for my mom. I liked it much better being on the inside looking out at the winter. I am still like that today during the winter months.

I remember one Saturday during the Christmas season my mom took my sister and me to see Santa Claus. He was appearing at a local department store. My sister and I were really excited to see Santa, but felt a little afraid at the same time. I remember sitting on his lap. He asked me if I had been a good girl, and, of course, I said "yes." As I proceeded to tell him what I would like, his long white beard fell off his face and onto my lap. I can still remember the commotion it caused for the "elves," and I remember a lady briskly trotting toward us with a roll of scotch tape, telling Santa to stay still while she taped his beard back onto his face. I sat on his lap the entire time. I was just five years old. After I left his lap and Santa promised I would get everything I asked for, my sister had her turn and I started to interrogate my mom

I asked her why Santa had a make-believe beard and whether the man in whose lap I'd sat truly was Santa at all. My mom told me that Santa is very busy and that he has helpers to help him. I remember thinking that this didn't seem like the right answer to my question. I remember asking how he got down the chimney, and I asked about the little children who don't have chimneys. *How does Santa get into their houses to give them their presents?* I remember having a lot of questions and not getting too many answers. I was full of suspicions. I had already heard rumors that there wasn't really a Santa Claus. I wasn't ready to accept that yet. I was only five and there still might have been a chance that there was a Santa. I remember always having doubts after that happened. Later, I liked making believe even when I knew for sure, trying to fool my parents into believing that I still believed. Then, I didn't know that they were always one step ahead of me. It was difficult to fool them but it didn't stop me from trying.

It was the same with the Easter Bunny. "Our" Easter Bunny seemed to know where to shop for the good candy. There was this candy store called "Putnam Pantry" that had the best candy in the world. Our Easter Bunny shopped there. Easter was fun because it occurred right after Lent. I was a "good" little girl so I would give up candy for Lent. By the time Easter came rolling along, I was indeed ready for a nice treat. I felt deserving of it because I followed the rules and made my sacrifices, including pretending for my younger siblings' sake. Childhood is made up of many make-believes and the Easter Bunny and Santa were a couple of them.

Some of my childhood memories are: my Chatty Cathy doll, flavor straws, my little red wagon, paper dolls, my Betsy Wetsy doll, singing "In the Alps" with my brownie troop, riding with my dad and mom to get chocolate chip ice cream, Cushman (a local company in our area) brownies, cheese sliced paper thin, Lena's (also a popular local shop) ham subs, seeing two movies (a news reel and a cartoon) at the local theatre for fifty cents, *Dennis the Menace, Life of Riley,* and *Wagon Train.*

I remember also writing a letter to the producers of *Queen for a Day* (hosted by Jack Bailey) for my mom to be honored and rewarded for all her pain and sacrifices. She never was chosen, but in my mind she should have been. I remember going to the mailbox to see if I would get a letter from the show. I felt she deserved it more than anyone. Lastly I remember counting the days to my summer vacation when I wouldn't have to worry about what would be awaiting me at school. These are some of the memories I have stored inside my memory bank.

Sometimes when I reflect on or see something that reminds me of my childhood, I often think of the way life was back then. I see how much life has changed and how life was so much simpler back then. I guess people of all generations probably could look back on their lives and say the same thing. Every new generation opens up a brand-new world filled with discoveries, joy, sadness, and beginnings.

Ma 25, Mommy + Pa 34 Tremblay

Nona's-Tony, Jeanne, Jacqui, Linda, Carol +Joey

Jacqui + Jeanne—Easter at Nona's

Nona + Mom

2

Mom

My mom was born in Salem, Massachusetts. She is the oldest of six children. A lot was expected of her because she was the oldest. She went to a French Catholic school where only French was spoken. She didn't speak English until she went to a public high school. French was spoken in the home and only French was allowed there as well. Her parents were extremely strict Catholics. Her whole family said the rosary every night on their knees after supper. My mother was a "good little Catholic girl." She obeyed all the rules, most of the time.

Once, my mom told us this story. In the mornings, she passed a farm on her way to school. One morning, she knew she was going to be late for school and she was going to be in *big* trouble. Regardless, she picked up a chicken egg that she found at the farm as she passed by and held it gingerly in her hand. As she entered the classroom she knew what was about to happen to her. Sure enough, the nun told her to put out her hand. As she unfolded her hand with the egg in the middle of it, the ruler came crashing down, hitting the raw egg. It went all over the place. The class laughed hysterically. The only two who weren't laughing were my mom and the nun. After meeting with my grandparents, the nun had my mother stay after school for a month. This was not the end of it; she paid the price at home, too. I believe she never tried a trick like that again. I asked her if she ever regretted doing that little stunt and she answered with a definite, "No, it was worth it!" This was a sure sign of her spunkiness and certainly not her last episode of it.

When my mom finished grammar school, she did not want to continue in a Catholic high school. Instead, she wanted to attend a school that offered courses such as typing, shorthand, and business. She convinced her parents that a public high school was the place for her. They did not feel that it was appropriate to send their daughter to a public school, but surprisingly, after much reflection, they agreed. Once in high school, my mom mastered the English language and learned all of the skills she had wanted. She made new friendships and grew into a lovely woman. She was known as being sweet and ladylike. She graduated from high school, gaining much confidence along with her knowledge. She was enjoying a brand-new world.

My mom didn't date much but she did have a few boyfriends before she met my dad. She was actually dating one of his friends before my parents began to date. She tells us that on one date her then-boyfriend took her to a dance. Later on that evening he brought my mom home and than sneakily went back to the dance to meet another girl. My mom found out broke up with him, and soon afterward started dating my dad. She didn't know if she liked him at first but that all changed when he pursued her. He sent her flowers and cards, and wrote her poems. She finally gave in and fell deeply in love with him. There was no turning back. They got engaged and were married during World War II. It was tough for both of them when they were separated (he was in the navy), but they had great dreams that together they were going to make it. She moved with him to Virginia where he was stationed, and although she was very homesick the love she shared with my dad comforted her. My mom later returned home and got a job after my dad was sent overseas. She then began anxiously awaiting his return.

Summer of 1944 Mom

At last, my dad returned from the service, and he started his own business. He built a masonry business that eventually turned out to be very lucrative but not until a lot of hard work, sacrifice, and sweat went into it. My mom worked hard, too, in the meantime. Together, they succeeded in accomplishing their dreams.

They wanted to build a home, and that they did. They moved from the city of Salem to a nearby town where my dad built us a beautiful brick house on thirteen acres of land. My mom enjoyed taking care of us and loved working in her rock garden and with all the beautiful flowers. It was a dream come true and it was their dream; however, this dream would not last.

I could never understand why my dad chose the path he did. My dad met another woman, fell in love with her, married her while my parents were still married and moved to another state. At this point in his heart he could not turn back. The only way he could survive with his conscience was to not have us in his life at all. This devastated our family and hurt many other people. He'd had no way of getting out of his situation; he had to choose, and he didn't choose us. It must have been difficult for him, and I believe that is why he never looked back; because if he had, he might have been tempted to stay. It was easier to walk away. This began a brand-new world for us all, and it would change us forever.

One thing I know for sure in my life is that my mother *always* loved me. I truly believe she was the "cement of my foundation." As a very young child I looked to my mom for guidance. I always felt safe with her. I knew she would protect me from the evil person I thought was lurking under my bed, or from the bad clown that haunted my head when I was asleep. Then, she held me and told me it was all a bad dream. Although it never felt like a dream at the time, she calmed my fears and made everything okay.

As I grew into early adolescence, we became "friends." It was at this time, I believe, that I took on the role of "husband" for my mom. I wanted her to be happy; but there wasn't anything that made her happy. I had a new mission: to protect my mom. If she could protect me, then I could protect her. I could save her from the kid down the street who threatened to throw tomatoes in her face when she opened the door. I was there to open the door instead of her. I was there to get the mail, and I prayed on the way to the mailbox that the child support check would be there. I was there to help her with her errands when her face broke out in a rash from nerves and she didn't want to be seen in public. I was there to take over. The fear I felt inside of me about running into some of the classmates that couldn't wait to bully me with their unkind words or gestures didn't matter anymore. I felt I had to take care of my mom. I wanted to make sure that no one would harm her.

My mom and I would listen for hours upon hours to country music that tore our hearts out, and yet, in a strange sense, gave us comfort. We played the entire tear-jerking albums of Tammy Wynette and Leroy Van Dyke in the darkness of our living room until the record literally turned white from use. We weren't alone, we could tell from the music; someone out there understood how we felt. They understood the pain. Could it be that someone else was suffering the same agonies that we were?

I look back now on how much I adopted my mom's feelings when I was a young girl. I tried to become her in hopes of taking her pain away. I was a child, but I could feel how an adult felt. She felt deserted, rejected, unloved, and lonely. I also felt deserted as a child. My mom didn't deserve what was dealt to her. In my wisdom, I knew that what had happened to her was never going to happen to me. I knew I never wanted to feel that pain again. Somehow I knew I could prevent it. I would never get married because I knew what could happen. Embedded in my haunting thoughts was, "Why should I ever get married?"

My mom was a wonderful person who took care of us and fed us. I never remember a night going to bed hungry or a cold winter night sleeping without heat. But I grew up too fast and the cuts were deep. My father left us when I was eleven years old. It is a very tender time for a child who is about to enter adolescence. It is an age when attachment to his or her parents is still very evident. I felt pain and sadness for my mom as if it were my own pain. I felt responsible for her. It was too much for any child to take on: I felt guilty if she wasn't happy, but no matter how I tried I couldn't make her happy.

From my parents' example, I truly believed that when two people got married, sadness and heartache is what they got. My mom was burdened with all the responsibility. It was up to her to save the family. She always made us feel that we were in "this thing" together. "Together until the end" was what we all decided to do. There was no other way. We only had each other so our broken family tried to mend, and eventually we did.

To me, marriage meant being left alone and trapped with all the responsibility of kids, taking care of a house, paying bills with the little money you had, and feeling depressed beyond words knowing your husband had found someone else in the meantime. My dad's infidelity cut my mother like a double-edged sword. All they worked for together; all those long, hard years of putting the business together ended in such unfairness. All their hopes, all their dreams, all their plans; were gone.

I feared how we would survive. We had each other. I had to make sure that my mom was going to be okay, because what would happen to us otherwise? I wanted her to stop crying. When she cried, I cried. She cried all the time; all day, all night. She was inconsolable. Fears of being separated from my sisters and brother reverberated in my head. I feared that my mom would not be able to afford to take care of us all. I feared that we would have to be put in those horrible foster homes. Maybe I watched too much television, but what happened to those families was not going to happen to us. I would not let it.

My mom often held family meetings. She asked us how badly we wanted to stay in our home. We all agreed that we wanted to stay in our home. She told us that contributing and doing our share would insure us having a place to live … a very nice place to live. We began to work together and formed a strong bond that would turn out to last a lifetime. I started babysitting, and when I was old enough to work I found a job to help my mom. My sister and I worked at a bakery for a while, and as we got older we moved on to other jobs.

The one thing I didn't feel I received from my mom was the support I needed from the trauma that I was experiencing in school. I wanted her so badly to believe the intensity of the pain I felt from the bullying and tormenting I was subjected to. She called me a martyr, and this hurt me. I don't know why she called me this. Perhaps she couldn't handle one more thing. Or, she might have been comparing her pain to mine and felt I had no reason to complain. I really don't know. I stopped crying, but only on the outside. I wanted my mother to *understand* my pain. I wanted her to believe me when I told her about what the kids at school were doing and saying to me. I felt so empty and so desperately alone. Although I felt my mom never believed me fully, I now understand that my mom was probably wrapped up in her own pain and had little energy to spare for me. One time, she did speak to the nuns, but that only made matters worse. Otherwise, she told me to ignore the kids in school, which I did, but it never worked. I know, though, that if she truly knew what I was going through, she would not have kept me in that school.

I prayed to God that when I came home from school that I would find her out of bed instead of in it in a deep depression. I wanted my mother back! I was getting exhausted trying to make things right, to no avail. I helped her with errands, gave her my hard earned babysitting money, did household chores, made her cards, gave her gifts and did anything else I could think of to see her smile. Nothing worked. Nothing! My mom didn't sleep during the night; instead, she cried. She did not work because she believed that a parent belonged home with her children. My brother was only eighteen months old when my father left. She feared for our safety and therefore, got little sleep.

After my dad left strange things started happening. We slept with the floodlights of our house on because of a fear of people lurking around our bedroom windows. In general, we feared for our lives. But we all knew that our mom was there to protect us. I always admired her for her bravery. She would "kill" before anyone hurt us.

My mom was a strict disciplinarian, and I was extremely obedient. We had a curfew until we were twenty-one. Yes, at twenty-one years old we had to be home by 12:00 a.m. We felt that since we were of legal age that we shouldn't have a curfew. Many of our friends had apartments or had parents who had no restrictions on them. Why should we? I started to venture out after I graduated from high school with some friends I had met at work. Nightclubs stayed open until 1:00 a.m. so I could never stay until the end. If I went with friends, they had to leave because I had a curfew. At midnight, my mom locked the door to the house.

I remember one time my sister got locked out of the house. She banged on the door to get in. My mom did not falter: my sister broke the rule, and she would pay. I couldn't stand to hear my sister crying so I got up, unlocked the door, and let her inside. I then had to add that to my "sin" list; I had disobeyed my mother. This sin was worth it because I "saved" my sister by turn.

My mom was full of grief and anger. One did not want to make her angry. She would lose complete control, so much so that she didn't even remember what had happened to make her so mad in the first place. My sister and I took over a lot of the responsibilities. My sister Jeanne especially worried about my brother's well being. She was thirteen and took on the heavy burden of worry. She remembers not wanting to go to school because she was afraid my mom wasn't well enough to care for our brother, John. My mom (and all of us for that matter) was in desperate need of counseling. Back in those days, people who went for counseling were usually considered mentally ill. Thankfully, times have changed. Then, though, she was overwhelmed. Looking back, I don't know how she ever managed to survive. She tells me it was for her children. We were all that mattered because she truly didn't want to live.

We all loved summertime; especially me, because I didn't have to attend school. We saved our pennies to go to an amusement park called *Pleasure Island* for our big end-of-the-summer event. It was so much fun, and our mom was so thrilled to take us. We also went for nice drives, stopping at the most unique places. We often stopped at a lake in New Hampshire and ate potato chips while sipping on a soft drink called Tab (in New Hampshire, stores were open on Sundays, and they were tax-free). It was fun, and it didn't cost much. We were together, and we were happy with that. My mom took us to the beach and to drive-in movies where we could wear our P. J's. We went to a place called "The Ritz" where they had the best cheap pizza in the world, and sometimes we would just go for a drive. Whatever the case we always found something to do together, and that was the best part of all. My mom wasn't crying for the moment, and we were all together. I tried my best not to think about school or how lonely I felt inside, because then I felt an emptiness that wouldn't let go of me.

I believe my mom felt she did her very best to give us what she could. Time has a way of healing, but some cuts are too deep to heal well. The layer over those cuts is thin and can be easily ripped open, but we manage to soothe the wound with the best four-letter word in the English language: LOVE.

My mom and I remain extremely close. We are true friends today. We travel together, hang out together, and help each other in any way we can. We are here for each other. She is a remarkable person who holds strength deep within her soul. She carries this strength that has held her through life's tragedies that no one person should ever have to bear. She is truly a survivor. The best part about it is that she is *my* mom. I can't imagine life without her.

3

Dad

One of my first memories is of my father. I remember I had fallen asleep in my dad's truck. As we approached our home, I remember making believe that I was still asleep so he could carry me inside. He carried me upstairs and sat me on the toilet seat where I proceeded to go to the bathroom, still asleep of course! He went right along with my little game. I wanted him all to myself. He was my dad and I loved him so much.

My dad was very talented and, although he never attended college, he was business smart. He loved his masonry work and took pride in it. He also became very successful. He was a workaholic, and to this day at 80 plus years is still working.

I remember when my dad was cementing the bricks together as he built our garage I asked him if I could help, and he proceeded to let me put cement on a brick and adhere it to another brick. I felt so proud to be working with my dad, and even happier that he allowed me to do so. I was six years old. I will always remember and be proud that I helped him build our house.

I know at one time I truly felt loved by my dad. He used to take us out for an ice cream after we left my grandma Nona's house. I remember sitting on the couch with him, watching television, and feeling so happy inside that he was *my* dad. I remember how hard he worked outside our house in our yard making it look absolutely beautiful, and I remember how I felt when I felt he loved me.

These may not seem to be remarkable events, but I remember them vividly. Little did I know that it would be these times I would carry in my heart throughout many years, for I would not have a relationship with my dad until much later.

Jacqui, Dad + Jeanne

In the beginning, my mom and dad got along fine, as far as I could see as a young child. But, it didn't last. They had horrendous fights, during which they verbally abused each other and I remember one of their huge fights as if it were yesterday. The fighting got so loud that my sister Jeanne joined me in my bed. We were shaking so much that my bed started to move on its casters. My brave sister Jeanne got up out of the bed and begged my mom and dad to stop. I will never forget that night. She yelled at my father bravely, though he got very angry with her. Still, she tried to stop him. She was afraid for our lives; we were just kids and we were so scared. It was a terrifying experience. They finally stopped fighting. I always felt badly that I couldn't be the one to tell them to stop. I think I was paralyzed with fear. I didn't know, at first, what it was; but something for sure was not right. Something terrible went wrong. Soon, I came to hear, but not really understand, that dad had fallen in love with another woman. It was time for him to leave; he left the house that night.

My mom bought this cute little doghouse plaque. On the dog's collar was a place to put the names of each member of the household. There was one for the mommy, one for the daddy, and one for each child. When a member of the household did something that wasn't considered good behavior that member ended up in the "dog house." We all took our turns in the doghouse for one reason or another, but we would often take it upon ourselves to decide who should spend sometime in the doghouse, too. After my dad left, we put him in the doghouse to stay. I felt that part of him was still with us, even if it meant that it was the part of him that was in the doghouse. Seeing his name, "daddy," gave me the sense that he still was a member of our family, and no one could steal that part of him from us.

I remember thinking that my siblings and I never wanted him to be buried, because our hope was that he would somehow want to join our family again. But, after my father left, our home had a sense of peace. The screams between my parents could no longer be heard. The fear of ending up with dead parents no longer tortured my mind. The pain in my heart, however, never went away. I longed for my parents to make amends. I wanted them to be happy, and I wanted our family to be together again. I started my crusade of praying to every saint I knew at the time; to reunite my mom and dad, to make it all better. I wanted my dad back the way it had been. The pain inside my heart and soul lingered on for months. Months turned to years and years turned to decades. Still I prayed, and still I hoped. It wasn't fair what happened. *It's not supposed to be like this*, I thought, over and over again, throughout the years.

My mom felt it was important to inform the nuns at school of our home situation; that my dad was no longer living with us. Shortly after my dad moved out, our furnace exploded. We were not there at the time, but because of the extensive damage we stayed at my grandmother's house in Salem. One morning, the Sister Superior came to my sister's and my classroom. She asked my sister Debbie and me to follow her. She told us that we had a visitor—our dad. I remember the nun staying close by while my father visited us. I remember going into the Sister Superior's office, and I thought that was pretty weird. No one was allowed in that room, never mind two little, unworthy children.

My dad wanted to know where we were staying. Somehow he had found out about the furnace accident. I felt as though I were in the middle. I didn't know if I was supposed to tell him where we were staying, but I wanted him to know where I was. I also wanted him to know how much I missed him and loved him. Although I didn't want the fighting between my parents to continue, I still held onto the hope that things could be different. I loved my dad, and prayed that my mom and dad would reunite. I told him where we were because in my heart I knew he wouldn't hurt us. However, I felt that I betrayed my mother and I couldn't wait to see her after school that day. I remember a deep sadness in my father's face then, or maybe that was what I wanted to see. Sadness meant that *maybe* he missed us and would return! It never happened. I remember feeling so, so sad, seeing my dad that day in school, and wanting to cry. I could find little words to say to him. What I wanted to say couldn't be spoken.

I remember so many disappointing incidents with my dad. One Fourth of July we waited for our dad to pick us up and bring us to a carnival. I remember being so excited that my sisters, brother, and I were going to be together with my dad. We waited at the picture window, but it continued to get later, and later, and later. Was he ever going to come? Did he forget? I can still feel the pain of losing hope that it would happen.

Well, he did come. It was 10:45 PM when he came down the driveway. He came in to get us. I remember the look on my mom and dad's faces. They said nothing, but I could hear their thoughts. He never did explain why he was late. I can't remember exactly how old I was, but I was probably around twelve years old. We hopped into his car and proceeded down Route One. When we arrived, the carnival was about to close. The bright lights that had shown from the highway slowly dimmed as we approached the parking lot. It was closing, and we were too late. We got an ice cream, and he took us home. I remember the silence on the way home and as we approached our beautiful, sprawling ranch house that he had built—that I had helped him build. As my dad drove down the two-hundred-foot drive, I wondered why the separation of my parents happened—I had no answer. I felt the emptiness in my heart again, wanting so much to be loved by my dad.

Many more disappointments occurred during the short time that my father was still in our lives. I remember one particular time that still saddens me today. We were always, always the last to get plowed out during a snowstorm. We lived far from the street. When I was in sixth grade, my Girl Scout troop went to a charm school that taught young ladies proper manners, including how to dress and walk properly. It was a six-week course, and was held on Saturdays. It took place on the third floor of a store called Filenes's. Our graduation from charm school was also held on a Saturday. It was the month of February and the weather was very unpredictable.

My mom had bought me a pretty dress and I was going to walk across the stage and get a diploma with the other girls. I had to be there at 10:00 AM sharp. The only problem was that it had snowed the day before and we had not been plowed out. There was no way my mom could get out of the driveway with over a foot of snow in her way. I was very upset. I could not believe I was going to miss my graduation. I had to make it. I wanted to walk across the stage, like all the other girls, to receive my diploma. I was eleven years old and I had been waiting for this day. I prayed so hard and at last a huge plow truck entered our driveway. The plow left at 9:55 AM. My mom and I jumped in the car and drove to the graduation. I remember walking into the room where the graduation was being held and being greeted by the hostess. Unfortunately they had already called my name. She made sure they called it again, and I walked down the runway and received my diploma; but it was too late. I was crushed. I remember wondering why we were always last to be plowed out. I didn't understand, and I felt no one cared about us. *Why didn't we matter? Why didn't anyone care?* I will never forget how I felt during that experience.

For a time, my mom would take us to my dad's workplace to see him. It was heart-wrenching for all of us. My mom waited in her cold car while we went to visit him in his ice-cold office. She felt it was important for us to have a relationship with him. I wasn't sure if he felt the same. I would sit there with a lump in my throat trying to figure out what happened. I missed my dad so much. The never-ending echo that rang in my head was that I wanted him to get back together with my mom. It was always a strange gathering, and I remember leaving feeling so distressed. I felt helpless in that situation. I felt empty and so confused, but I still held onto a thread of hope that maybe my parents could still work it out and get back together. I didn't even know what to talk about with my dad, so consumed was I by my thoughts, a continuous gnawing of deep sadness. My dad would ask us how school was and he also occasionally asked us about our mom. This only gave me hope, and I was always instantly so anxious to tell my mom that he asked about her. I knew that this would make her smile. The visits were short and lacking of comfort, however.

I do remember seeing clothes hanging on a hook outside of his office door. I wanted to believe that he didn't really have someone else and that he was living there. I knew it could be possible, because there was a small kitchen where he could cook and a couch where he could sleep. I wanted to believe this so badly, but in my heart I think I knew I was only wishing it could be true. I remember telling my mom to give her hope that maybe he would come back, and that maybe he didn't have someone else after all. After a while, the visits stopped, and the times in between seeing my dad turned into years.

So many things cloud my mind about my dad, and yet I always wanted to believe he still did love us. I tried so hard to understand why he left. Why didn't we matter to him? I felt after a while that he didn't love us anymore, and that hurt, razor deep. I knew even at my young age that this would haunt me for many years. It did. I wanted him to love me, and it wasn't fair that he chose someone over us. I felt as if he had been stolen, but of course it had been his choice. It wasn't fair that we had to live without a dad, though. How could it have happened? Why weren't my prayers being answered? I prayed harder and never stopped until years later when it didn't make a difference anymore. I had to go on with my life without him instead. I felt so empty inside, and I am sure that the kids who bullied me easily picked up my insecure vibes.

As I got older I still had to know why; why did my father leave? I was into my thirties and still got a lump in my throat whenever I visited my dad. I still felt as if I was thirteen years old. As I grew into adulthood, I saw my dad very infrequently except for a yearly visit at Christmas time. Our short conversations changed from "How is school?" to "Jacqui, when are you getting married?" I wanted to scream at the top of my lungs to him, *"Never, Daddy, never! I feel robbed of my trust. I will never trust anyone. Why would I want to marry? Look what happens!"*

I thought about asking my dad about what happened between my mom and him for him to make such a drastic decision in his life, a decision that would affect more than just him. I just had to get up the nerve. I was afraid he would reject me; but then again, I already felt that way, anyway. I decided I didn't have anything to lose. I remember one day I phoned my dad. I wanted to see him. He agreed to meet with me at his work. I had written him a letter explaining how I felt as a child and as an adult today. I would bring it with me. I would know by the end of our visit whether or not I would leave the letter. I decided it was only fair to hear his side of the story. I was hoping this would help me understand more clearly. I needed to know why he stopped loving us—why, why, why? I had a deep hole in my heart and I wanted it to heal.

I took a deep breath and asked him what had happened. I kept in mind that I would not defend my mother. I let him speak. I felt I owed him that. It had taken me over twenty years to muster up the courage, but there I was, finally sitting face-to-face with my "daddy." True to my resolve, I never said a word. I let him talk. I left there without the letter, and I left feeling very sad. They had both been so unhappy. They had both been so very young when they had married and started their family, still searching for what was missing in their lives. My father chose to leave and start a new life, but we all were sacrificed because of it.

Seventeen years after he left home, my mother and father finally divorced in 1977. It set my dad free from my mom, but I often wonder if it set him free from himself. Deep inside, I love my dad. I long to this day for a father who truly cared for me as he had done so long ago when I was a very young child. Time has passed but I guess I never really let go of wanting a daddy to call my own. My dad has mellowed through the years. He is much older now and has health problems but still continues to work. I have found peace with him. I still see him during the Christmas season and occasionally during other times. I want to believe that if he had to do it over again he would not make the same choices, but that's probably the kid in me talking.

Dad + Mom 12-01-1943

Mom, Dad + **Nona**

4

Strange Happenings

Many unusual incidents occurred shortly after my father left our home. One morning, as my mom started her car, she heard a big "boom." Suddenly, her car started to smoke. She immediately got out of her car. She didn't know what to think, or what was happening, for that matter. She called the police who came to our house to investigate. Evidence of a cherry bomb was found near the car. This could have exploded the gas tank and the results could have been horrific. Why? Why would someone do such an awful thing? Why would anyone want to bring harm to her or our family? It was an awful experience. Did my mom have any enemies? I remember even thinking that someone was out to get *me*. Was it known that we were now alone? I was afraid for the longest time to get into our car. What would happen if it blew up with all of us inside of it? We could all get killed. What would happen if my mom got killed? What would we do? We already lost a dad; we couldn't lose our mom, too! Who would do this? We never did find out.

On several nights, also during that time, we heard footsteps outside of our bedroom windows. The footsteps were very close. We were quite far from the street so it was definitely not a person just passing by on the sidewalk. I remember lying in bed one summer and hearing footsteps that seemed to be right under my window's ledge. It was too warm inside the house, but I was so afraid that I quietly and slowly closed the window when the footsteps disappeared. I was too scared to leave the window open even a crack. I was petrified that someone would break in and kill us. I went through many sleepless nights wishing I could go to sleep with my mom in her bed. Unfortunately, there were four of us, not including her, and we all had the same thought, so there was no room to be had. My mom had always assured us that she would protect us, but who was going to protect *her*? She wanted us to feel safe, but she herself didn't feel safe. Someone was stalking our house, and we didn't know who or why. We were scared. Maybe I was imagining the intruder. Maybe the others were, too. I truly wanted to believe that. We were so vulnerable. We were so alone.

My mom was quite the detective, and one morning she found a cigarette butt, half smoked, and a disturbed bush. These were sure signs that someone had been there—but who? We felt unsafe in our own home. The cherry bomb was scary enough, but now this? I would wake up in the middle of the night thinking someone was trying to get into my bedroom. I slept with the light on many nights. We would leave the house floodlights on at night for safety. Maybe it was a sense of false security, but it seemed to help a little anyway.

My mom had had enough, though, and ended up calling the police again. I remember they listened to what she had to say and promised her that they would patrol the area diligently. They did patrol for a while, as I remember seeing the patrol car slowly pass by our home, but then they were gone. After awhile they stopped coming because evidently they found nothing conclusive. I remember being so afraid that I would tremble. I was afraid for my mom and afraid that someone was trying to harm her. How awful it would be to lose our mother consumed my thoughts. I remember praying for God to protect all of us, but especially my mom.

I got home from school one day to find our beautiful home covered with soot everywhere. That was the time that our furnace had exploded. My mom had no money for emergency repairs. Our clothes were ruined and the curtains and drapes were the color of black coal. The walls were grayish in color with tinges of black that looked like huge smudge marks. It was scary. We couldn't stay at our home. My mom called my dear grandmother in Salem, and she welcomed our coming with open arms, as she always did. We moved to my grandmother's until my mom could settle with the insurance company. I enjoyed staying with my grandmother and I felt safe—we all did. I loved being with my grandmother and I remembered how I had felt when I lived upstairs from her so very long ago. It's funny, but then I really didn't miss my home.

After a thorough investigation by the inspector my mom was told that the explosion to the furnace was due to tampering and not because of a malfunction. Who was doing this? Was this happening to us because someone knew we were alone? Who knew there wasn't a man around the house? Or was something else going on? This frightened us. Could it be that someone was trying to hurt us? Who? Who would want us dead? This went on for about two years after my dad left and then it suddenly stopped, but the fear still lingered with us. My brother was just about two years old, my younger sister was seven, I was twelve, and my older sister was fourteen when this occurred. We were young and we were scared.

We as a family became even closer and we never let each other be alone, nor did we want to be. We needed each other and we certainly loved each other. After all we only had each other.

No one was ever connected to any of these incidents, and my mom didn't have the energy to try to find out who may have been behind them, but the fear that overwhelmed us continued for quite some time. My mom would lay awake all night, which would explain one of the reasons why she was always in bed when we got home from school. This always bothered me. I wanted her so badly to be up and about so I could share my day with her, which was never very good. I needed her to be there for me. I wanted her to comfort me from the hellish day I had just experienced. I felt so alone and so empty. I didn't know how I could fill the emptiness that lurked inside of me; it was an emptiness that would not let go. Meanwhile, fear encompassed my entire being.

I felt resentful that my mom was sure to be in bed whenever I got off the school bus. Why couldn't my life be happy like everyone else's? I wondered when things would get better or if they ever would. I began to wish my life away. As each day passed, I was happy only that another week was closer to coming to an end. I prayed each night not to awaken in the morning. I wanted to die. I wanted to die, and hopefully be with Mary the Mother of God in heaven. I would then be able to ask Mary if she could take my mother up to heaven so she would be happy. I knew she would be happy in heaven, and then, and only then, would I feel happy. I remember hearing in school that we should pray to Mary to ask her Son for favors because Jesus, her Son, would never say no to His mother. I prayed and prayed and prayed, and even though I truly believed that Mary could hear me, I felt my prayers were not going to be answered for a long, long time. I needed to earn my wings. I had it all figured out, but it never happened. I woke up each morning with the fear of the day still ahead of me. My fears always turned into reality, and again, after a horrendous day at school, I would get off the school bus, walk down our long drive into our house … to a mom who didn't want to live.

5

Neighborhood

I lived in a very simple neighborhood on a quiet street. I hated my town. Doesn't everybody? I couldn't wait to grow up and move away from it. I didn't have much fun. I didn't even know how to have fun. I couldn't wait to move to a place where no one knew me and I could have a new start.

Beginning school again in the fall was quite scary to me after the summer routine. I didn't know what to expect. First of all, I had to get up in the morning and get dressed. I could no longer stay in my pajamas and be with my mom. I remember my mom always tried to get me to eat breakfast before I left for school in the morning. I wasn't ever hungry and I never wanted to eat, though. She made me eat or at least have something to drink. She was pretty persistent about that. She felt it was important for children to have something in their stomachs so they could learn better.

The only way she could make sure that I got my so-called nourishment was to make me eggnog. She would put a raw egg in a glass, add milk and vanilla, and beat the concoction with a fork. She would then make me drink it down. She told me it was good for me and would make me strong. This was the one and only way she could get me to eat breakfast, or an egg for that matter. I think I drank it just to make her happy. I never was a breakfast eater because I was much too nervous even to think of eating breakfast. I would walk up the driveway to the school bus sick to my stomach from fear and anxiety. I would throw up in the driveway and end up crying. I was so upset anyway, and forcing myself to eat breakfast just added to my stress. My mother finally agreed that breakfast did not agree with me, and she no longer made me put something in my stomach. It didn't stay there anyway. It left me with a stomachache.

Some of the same kids who harassed and bullied me at school unfortunately lived in my neighborhood. I would get on the bus and often sit by myself if my friend Tina didn't take the bus that day. I would hear voices whisper that I had cooties, and weird sounds such as oinking came toward me. Somehow they seemed to keep their voices quiet enough not to call any attention to the bus driver. Occasionally he would yell at the kids on the bus to "knock it off" for whatever reason at the time. I was called slur words such as the N word, scab, scuzz, fatty to my face and they would stick their feet into the aisle hoping that I would fall. Fortunately these kids did not wait at the same bus stop as me. In fact, my bus stop was directly at the top of my driveway so I didn't have far to go. I would often see my mom looking out our large picture window as if she was shielding me from any harm. After I got on the bus, though, the shield was no longer there. I always tried to sit in a seat at the front of the bus but this was not always possible. I wanted to be invisible. I wanted to disappear. I wanted to cry, and at the beginning I often did cry.

My older sister Jeanne went to a different school so she wasn't on the same bus. My younger sister Debbie was five years my junior so did not ride the bus when I did, either. My brother Johnny was an infant; by the time he attended school I was in high school. I was afraid to sit in the back of the bus, because most of the taunts came from there. We had a really nice bus driver who would greet me joyfully as I stepped onto the bus, and wish me a good day as I stepped off the bus, but who never took authority with those in the back of the bus. I continued to have stomachaches every morning. After continually being ill, my mother took me to the doctor. He couldn't find anything wrong. I was hospitalized for tests and the results were: "nerves." I was extremely stressed.

Most of the houses on our street were quite modest in size except for our house and the houses of my two cousins. I lived next door to my cousin Tony, and he lived next door to my other cousin Carol. Our parents together bought nine acres of land. They divided it among them equally giving each family three acres. Eventually my parents bought an additional ten acres of land. The land was originally called "The Pines" because of the beautiful pine trees that graced the land. My home had a huge back yard that had ten apple trees, five peach trees, and a big old pine tree that stood, literally, one-hundred-feet high. The pine tree was beautiful.

Our house was two hundred feet from the street and featured a beautiful rock garden in the middle of a huge area surrounded by a horseshoe driveway. My mom religiously took great pride in beautifying it. It had all kinds of lovely flowers, including phlox, pansies, and daffodils. We had pretty shrubs in front of each of the windows that added to the beauty of the house. Roses graced the property in bright yellows, pinks, and reds. The post and rail fence surrounding our property made it look like a true ranch. Shrubs along the fence also added to the landscape. It was indeed beautiful. I was proud and thankful to live there.

I felt that some of the kids were jealous of where I lived, and in my heart I was happy that I had this one thing that they didn't. Our backyard abutted the woods and was very private. We were comfortable sitting out in the backyard in our pajamas, and even running out in the yard in our slips to feed the dog, sheep, goats, and my sister's bunny. We could have private conversations where no one could hear us. It was great, and a wonderful escape from the busy world outside.

We had a huge living room, a den area, and an eat-in kitchen. My mom had bought a red horseshoe-shaped booth and a kitchen table. We all thought that the set-up was pretty neat; no one else had a booth to sit at while eating dinner. We often made believe we were at a restaurant. I was always the waitress. I made menus and passed them out to the patrons (my sisters). I would make them what they ordered off the menu and serve it to them. It was fun, probably more fun for them. It didn't matter, though; I liked doing it. Our house had three bedrooms, one of which was a master bedroom with its own bathroom. Then there were two children's rooms, which shared a full bath. My little brother had to share a room with my younger sister. He was very young so it didn't matter at first. Eventually when my older sister moved out, my younger sister moved into my room and my brother John got to have a room of his own. Our basement was completely finished with a kitchen and another bath. Our house had three fireplaces: one in our living room, one in our breezeway, and one in our basement. All were workable fireplaces. We had a two-car garage that connected to the breezeway. It looked like we had it all from the outside, but such a house was a tremendous up-keep for my mom; however, we all pitched in, dutifully completing our chores.

Our home was not completely finished in the first years we lived there, but my parents worked hard to complete the final touches. We loved our animals, and we certainly had enough room for them. My dad put up a wire fence to keep them from escaping, and they scampered about in a playful way. I particularly remember the goats. One was named Calico because of his brown, black, and white spots, and then there was Star because he had a star in the middle of his forehead. Calico was my favorite. He was small, a baby. The goats loved eating grain from our hands. My sisters and I loved our pets. The ram, on the other hand, was rambunctious. He was actually very mean and chased the sheep. He pushed them away from the trough where they tried to eat their grain, not letting them near it.

Our dog Heidi was a German Shepherd, and she did not like our sheep. One evening when we were asleep she jumped the fence and killed one of them. I remember going out to feed the animals in the morning, and found the dead sheep's body severed; its neck was ripped open and its head was lying in the trough. I was very upset. My dad decided to give Heidi away. He told us she went to live on a farm in New Hampshire. I remember my dad putting Heidi in the car and driving away. A couple of days went by, and to our surprise, we found Heidi in our backyard again. This was amazing.

Our Home

Our Farm Animals-Star, Calico, Ram + Sheep

She had actually found her way back to our house. My dad brought her to the farm in New Hampshire again. The owner said that they could train Heidi to round up the sheep and be useful on the farm. This time she did not return. I am not sure how they managed to keep her from returning, but, whatever they did, it worked. We were not sad to see her depart. She was not a "family" dog; at least not for our family.

My parents eventually sold all of the farm animals, and we got a new dog. Jet was a full-breed cocker spaniel, and we loved her. She was jet black, which explains her name. She was five weeks old when she came to live with us. We were thrilled. She had a great temperament. She was gentle and playful. She never grew to be a large or a tall dog. She weighed about fifteen pounds. We loved her and were sad when she passed away at thirteen. Through the years we had cats, dogs, rabbits, birds, fish, and guinea pigs, in addition to our other animals. Eventually, as we all got older, we decided we had enough problems taking care of ourselves, let alone pets.

During my childhood, I spent lots of my free time with my animals, but I did find some friends to play with, too. Thumbing through a magazine one day, I came across an article about an orphanage and school for Indian boys and girls. The name of the school was St. Joseph's Indian School. They were asking for donations to help fund the school and provide food, housing, and school supplies for the children. I felt badly for them and I wanted to help in any way I could. I asked my friend Tina about starting a club of our own. We wanted more than two members, though, so we asked our neighborhood friend Marie if she wanted to join. She was a little younger than Tina and me and had her own friends, but she agreed, and we were glad that she accepted the "nomination." We met in my basement. Dues were collected each week until we felt we had collected enough money to send to the school. Dues were twenty-five cents each week. Each of the three of us was more than happy to contribute to this great cause. To this day I still get their newsletter, and on occasion I send them a donation.

Tina and I loved to play at my house. It was huge, for one thing, and it was private; so we had lots of room to listen to records, color, play games, and be creative. I had the biggest yard, and in it we could have our own little corner of the world. We usually "escaped" to my basement. There was privacy there, too. There was also a bathroom that I didn't need permission to use. We loved it. We would make things, tell stories, sing our little hearts out, and say our prayers together. We would end our playtime with snacks, which my mom always prepared for us.

Tina and I were inseparable. Marie, our friend and club member, was nice and kind. These two friends were a great escape for me from the neighborhood bullies who continued to antagonize me as I walked down the street, calling me names and shouting hurtful words with vengeance in their hearts. I learned from them that my olive complexion would haunt me for my entire life. Or this was what I believed, anyway. It was "bad" to have dark skin. I wasn't "as good" as others. I truly believed this. Aiming spit at me, and calling me the *n* word, scab, pig and anything else that they could think of to offend me was a regular ritual with them. They hated me, and it seemed it was for no reason at all except for the fact that my skin tone was darker than theirs. I never wanted to venture out on my own, for fear of them.

I seldom went out after school anyway, because I didn't want to leave my mother. I did go out with Tina on Saturdays to eat at the local diner. Tina and I saved our babysitting money, and this was our "treat." I loved going to the diner. It was fun, and I felt pretty grown up going to a restaurant with a friend and ordering whatever I wanted. Tina and I usually got a hamburger and French fries or onion rings. Yum! This was until I discovered the calorie book.

Aside from my diner outings, though, I was scared to wander in the neighborhood. One boy in particular scared me the most. I had to pass this boy's house to reach any destination. It was almost as though he were looking for me. He always seemed to be outside when I passed by. I never walked alone because I was afraid that he and his friends would hurt me, physically, or with their cruel words. As much as I tried to ignore their unkind words I could not help but feel pain and I wondered why they got so much pleasure from it.

Our neighborhood harbored a deep, dark secret that was not discovered until much later and much too late for many people including my own family. Years later I was told about an article in a local paper about closing an artesian well in the area, from which we received our water. It stated that the chemicals seeped into the well and polluted and poisoned our water supply. Could this have been the cause of the cancer that ravaged our neighborhood? All types of cancer had emerged, from brain cancer to leukemia. We had no idea of the nightmares that were about to happen to our own family. Our own experience with cancer is discussed in detail in later chapters.

One evening my sister Jeanne returned from work with devastating news. The woman she worked with in our neighborhood had a brain tumor. Soon thereafter, she no longer was able to work. The doctors tried to save her, but it wasn't long until she passed away. Cancer then continued to plague the residents of our street and surrounding neighborhood. Shortly after the death of Jeanne's co-worker we heard that a young boy around age thirteen had developed cancer in his leg. He lost his leg, and eventually, his life. The cancer incidents continued to grow. My brother suffered from the catastrophic illness of leukemia, which is cancer of the blood. It took his life when he was only thirteen. Five years later, cancer almost took my life, too. Cancer struck me when I was twenty-six. I had a very rare type of cancer that grew as a tumor in my left leg. It was only because of the great doctors, especially my primary care doctor who researched my case, and divine intervention that I am here today. Indeed it is a miracle that I survived.

Years after I was afflicted with this dreadful disease, another neighbor died of cancer. This death was particularly hard, because the woman who died had been my girlfriend Marie's mother, who had been so kind in helping me through my own ordeal. A sweet lady, she often came to help me during the weeks I had my chemotherapy. My mom had to work and I really needed someone by my side. She was there. She was diagnosed with brain cancer and cancer of the esophagus. She suffered a lot and succumbed to the disease quickly. Her son (Marie's brother) had died years earlier of brain cancer. They had lived in the same house together. Shortly after this tragedy, my best friend Tina's mother died from breast cancer. Many, too many, cancer episodes for one small neighborhood were more than just coincidence. It had gotten way out of hand. My cousin Tony, who lived next door to us, developed a rare type of cancer and had to go for rigorous treatments. He was one of the lucky ones who survived. His mother was not so lucky. She developed lung cancer and died in 1998.

On a lighter note, our neighborhood was also a place for some fun and interesting adventures. My sister Jeanne and I made necklaces and rings out of colored gimp (plastic string-like material). This took skill, and we were very proud of ourselves when we were finished with our masterpieces. It was a fun pastime. Each fall, we walked two houses down from ours in the opposite direction of the mean boys to gather up pignuts and chestnuts that had fallen from the trees. We cracked them open with rocks that we found along the way. The "meat" inside the pignuts was succulent. There was hardly any substance to these nuts—they never ruined our suppers—but they tasted delicious, and it was fun finding and enjoying them. I remember I liked breaking the green, porcupine-like covering of the chestnuts open only to discover a bright, shiny, brown nut inside each one. I didn't like eating these nuts, but I loved collecting them.

I remember one day Jeanne and I ventured out into the woods. We were going to be really brave, and see if we could reach the other side of the woods that led to the parallel street. I was familiar with that street because the bus route went along it to bring us to school. We would know how to get home from there, we reasoned. It seemed like we had been walking forever when we came across an old cemetery. The headstones were battered and the etching on each stone was barely readable. It was actually a cemetery from the 1800s. We found it interesting that a brightly colored American flag was propped up on the side of each gravestone stone. *Who could have been here, putting these flags by the grave markers?* We asked ourselves. No one would believe us if we told them about our find. We decided we would bring back proof. My sister and I each took a flag and presented them to our mom. Her reaction surprised us. First, she was upset with us for venturing so far from our house. Secondly, she told us that a cemetery was very sacred, and that it was stealing to take the flags. This was just what I needed: something else to add to my list of sins. We had to bring the flags back. *Could we find that place again?* We wondered *Would she allow us to go to the cemetery?* Surprisingly she did. I am sure that she was quite worried until we returned home, but we did retrace our steps and returned the flags to their proper places. We never went there again.

A section of our neighborhood was called "The Pines," and a huge stand of pine trees was still there, shading a lone road that led to an old, dilapidated house. In this house lived one "old" man who was said to have had a shotgun. He didn't like children at all, and whenever we came close to his house he would chase us away. It was very adventurous trying to see how close we could approach his shack without him catching us. If he saw us as he opened up his door we knew it was time to run as fast as we could. Our lives were at stake; at least this is what we believed. Eventually that land was sold and he moved out of town.

There was also an abandoned house down the street from us. It was truly haunted, or so we thought. It was said that someone got killed in the house and they never left. We imagined we heard ghostly noises throughout the house when we snuck into it. The basement had a dirt floor and fieldstone walls. We bravely worked our way down the warped and broken wooden staircase to it. We always stayed together when exploring in the big old house. A partially hidden door peeked out from a dilapidated wall, which, when opened, made an eerie creaking noise and led to a secret staircase. The house itself was up a long driveway that was surrounded by overgrown bushes that added to the mystique of the place.

This mysterious house had a library room with very old books that were probably quite valuable, but I didn't feel right taking any so I never did. As we explored each and every room of the house, we became more spooked, just by the creaks that came from our steps on the old wooden floors. Each room had its own mystique. The tall pine trees shadowing the house, set back on a hill from the street, created a feeling that nothing lurked inside of the house but evil. It had been somewhat vandalized over the years, and had broken windows and damaged walls. The grass had not been cut in a very long time and the lawn was totally covered in weeds. A sign at the bottom of the driveway warned everyone not to trespass.

I loved the adventure and the mystery of the whole place. It added a little excitement to my life. One day, when we went back to revisit the old house, we saw a sign that stated the property was sold. This time, we knew we should not even contemplate entering the house. The house was totally demolished and a new home was built, and so our adventures in the haunted house ended.

I never ventured outside of my neighborhood. We lived three miles from town but my mom never thought that dropping us off at the "square" was proper so we didn't loiter in town. The kids who hung out in town got in trouble, and my mom would not allow that to happen to us. With the exception of Brownies and Girl Scouts once a month, we really didn't do much else as far as extra-curricular activities. Everything that was offered was at a driving distance, and it was too difficult for my mom to drive us to all the different places at all the different times, so she didn't do it. I would have liked to escape from the neighborhood for a while, but it didn't happen. I was just hoping and praying for the day I no longer had to live in the town. As I look back now, I find that I actually like the town. The demons, of the neighborhood for the most part, are packed away forever to stay.

Debbie 10 yrs old + Johnny 5 yrs old in our backyard

6

Grammar School

I entered school in September of 1956. I was quite afraid of going to school. I enjoyed being home with my mother. I wanted to stay with her and be her pal. I was her little girl and she was my mommy, but the reality was that this could not go on forever. I had to go to school. Reluctantly, I moved on to the big, wide world of first grade.

I remember well my first grade teacher, Mrs. B. She was so nice and very grandmotherly. I always wanted to please her and do the very best I could. I was very small for my age and a young six-year-old. I missed my mother and school was tiring and difficult. The harder I tried, the more difficult it was. I remember practicing writing my name over and over again. I had a long name, and as I tried to print each letter, I got more frustrated that they were not coming out perfectly. I spent hours after school and on weekends at home printing the alphabet; first the capitals, and then the "little ones." They were long school days and I was glad when they were over.

Back in those days, we didn't have a cafeteria or hot lunch so we brought our lunch from home. They did serve milk, and it cost three cents for an individual carton. We usually brought in our milk money at the beginning of the week—a total of fifteen cents. Wow—prices sure have changed! My mom always made me a lunch to bring to school. If we had eaten hamburger sandwiches for supper, and there was some left over, my mom would pack one up for my lunch. One particular day, Mrs. B. saw my sandwich during lunch and noted how big and thick it was. She called the second grade teacher over to see my hamburger. Next, all of the children gathered around to see my sandwich. I felt so embarrassed. I went home to tell my mother never to give me a hamburger sandwich like that again. She thought it was funny, *ha, ha*! Unfortunately, I could not run away from home to my grandmother's this time.

The hamburger sandwiches wouldn't stop coming, but I knew what I could do about them. There was a friendly dog in the schoolyard. Each morning, he greeted the children. He was a big black dog, or at least he appeared to be big. (He was probably small, but since we were little children everything appeared big to us.) We all played with him until we had to go on inside for school. The next time we had hamburgers for supper, I knew that afterward I would surely find the leftovers in my lunch box. That next morning, just as I expected, I saw a hamburger sandwich when I opened the box. But, I had a plan. I paid a special visit to the dog before going inside with the other children that morning. When lunchtime came along, I told Mrs. B. that I had lost my lunch. She asked the class for volunteers to share their lunch with "poor little Jacqui." Even if they gave me what they didn't like, at least I didn't have to go through the embarrassment of having that gigantic hamburger in front of me again!

One of my other memorable experiences from grammar school is of the first time we had an eye test. I wanted to pass so badly. All the kids were talking about an apple on the table so I knew that would be something I had to locate. When my time for the test came, sure enough, the woman who was the "tester asked me the question, "Jacqui, is the apple on the table?" Well, darned if I could find the apple on the table! I suppose I should have been glad I saw the table, but honestly, I did not see that apple for the life of me. I knew it had to be there, though, because the other kids all said they saw it. Perhaps it rolled off the table by the time it was my turn. Anyway, I sheepishly said, "yes." I think the "tester" picked up on my hesitance so she asked me where the apple was on the table. When I couldn't tell her, I was sent home with a note for my mother to take me to an eye doctor for an eye exam. My mother made an appointment with the eye doctor. I knew there was no way of fooling a doctor. Of course I needed glasses. I remember crying because I didn't want glasses. I was afraid that everyone would laugh at me. My mother let me pick out my own frames. They were red plaid. She tried to talk me into something plain, but if I were ever to wear those things then I wanted to get my own choice. So I did. Wearing them turned out to be another thing. My mother told me I looked beautiful in them. "How can I look beautiful in glasses?" I scoffed.

I remember walking to the bus stop wearing my glasses for the first time. I got on the bus and I felt all the kids staring at me. I felt awful, because, sure enough, that very first day the kids laughed at me and commented how awful I looked, asking me why I couldn't see and had to wear glasses. *Forget it! No more glasses!* I took them off, put them in my school bag, and there they stayed until I got off the bus and put them on again for my trip down the driveway. I hardly wore them again, especially in school.

School held one trauma after another for me. I was in a new town, my grandmother was far away, and I had to leave my mother behind me. Also, the sixties were years of many prejudices. If you looked different than the stereotypical American—white, blond hair, blue eyes—then you were easy prey. This was the beginning of a small seed that would progress like a cancerous growth. I was white, I felt; however, my olive skin was different to them, and that was all they needed. Their attitudes changed my life and how I felt about myself. I began to believe that there was something "bad" about not being light-skinned. My first real taste of prejudice was when a first grader called me the "N" word. He was really mean, and although I wasn't sure what was so bad about that "N" word I knew by the tone in his voice that it was bad. He did not like me and I was somehow different. Looking back, I wonder if he even knew what the word he used meant. However, it didn't matter to him; his intent was to hurt me, and he did.

The year ended and I moved on to second grade. What was second grade going to be like? Was it going to be the same? Was it going to be better? I had heard that the second grade teacher was really nice, and as little as I knew about her she seemed nice. Anyway, summer came and went, and in September of 1957 I went back to school. I did like my second grade teacher. In fact, I remember her now as my favorite teacher. Her name was Mrs. H. I felt she really liked me. I felt safe when she was around me. I was small and immature for my age still, and I needed to feel the security of an older adult. I made it through second grade without any huge crisis, but still experienced the cruelness of how kids can often be.

A new Catholic school had been built in the area, meanwhile, and it was taking applications for admission in the fall of 1958. My mom felt that this would be a better school for me to attend. The tuition at the time was thirty dollars a year as unbelievable as it seems today that was the actual cost. This was more than my mom could afford. She visited the admissions office at the school and explained her financial situation and her strong desire to have me attend. One day, a letter of acceptance arrived in the mail. The following year I entered the third grade, and would begin a journey that would affect my entire life.

7

Catholic School

Little did I know what I was in store for me when I transferred to a new school as a third grader! The new Catholic grammar school opened its doors and I walked in, immediately finding it quite different than public school. I had been excited to go to a new school, even though I still really hadn't wanted to leave my mom. But, I'd been glad for the chance to get away from that other school with the mean kids. The nuns wore floor-length, black habits with white bands of cloth that covered their foreheads. Rosary beads circled their waists loosely. In their hands the nuns carried clickers that we didn't want to see or hear. They were soldiers of God, and they were all going to heaven because they had given up their lives for God. So we were told.

They were very strict, to say the least. I wore a uniform that consisted of a gray jumper, white blouse, red knee socks, and red bow. Our shoes had to be tie shoes and certainly could not be of patent leather. We often had dress inspection, and God forbid if a spot or wrinkle was found on our uniform, bow, or blouse! Our knee socks could not fall to our ankles, and if they did this infraction warranted a "blue" demerit slip, which meant detention or extra homework. The demerit slip had to be signed by a parent and returned, and this was the *worst*. In addition, our shoes had to be polished but absolutely could not be shiny. Polish was a sin.

I learned a lot the first few years I attended Catholic school. The "truths" included: the Catholic religion was the *only* "true" religion, only the really good people such as the nuns would go to heaven, and we would go to hell unless we prayed, and prayed, and prayed and did penance for God. If we were to be saved, we had to obey the rules and be humble. We had to say rosary after rosary and many novenas kneeling on the floor by our chairs. Priests were to be revered and they could do no wrong. They were put on a very high pedestal.

There were many rules and regulations of being a "good" Catholic. I learned about mortal sins and venial sins. Mortal sins were deadly, and assured you of the burning fires of hell, where it would be hot and there would be no water to drink.

Venial sins were little sins and, although you weren't promised hell if you committed these, you would have to go to a place called purgatory. The burning flames were the same, and there wasn't any water there, either; but you were definitely not there to stay. You could lessen your stay by praying, saying multitudes of little ejaculations (small prayers) (and yes, that is what they were called), or by doing good deeds. There was hope.

I was going to make sure that I wasn't going to hell. I was going to *pray, pray, pray* and find prayers that offered the most indulgences. Nuns, priests, and martyrs had a gold ticket. My mom and grandmother were wonderful and good in my eyes. They sacrificed much for their children and gave up many things in order to provide for them. They would go, too. I knew that only the nuns, priests, martyrs, my mom, and my grandmother were going straight to heaven, but at least I had a lifetime to pray and be good to take years off my sentence.

At the beginning of the school day we proceeded to our classroom after lining up in the schoolyard. Boys lined up on one side, and girls queued up on the opposite side of a marked line. We didn't even think of crossing the line. We slowly walked to the door of the school but did not enter until the sound of the bell. We walked to our designated classrooms where we stood at attention. We then said morning prayers and the Pledge of Allegiance. This was the way the beginning of every school day went. The nun checked to make sure we were properly dressed and we girls didn't forget to wear our bright red bows, or the boys their bright red ties. If there were any sounds except for the sounds of our voices praying, the nun would use her clicker to get our attention. I could not even count the times that we heard that clicker: *click, click, click*!

We prayed for peace and prayed that a bomb would not hit our country. I remember we had air raid drills. They were pretty scary. We had to get under our desks and put our hands on our heads and pray. I remember asking my guardian angel to protect my mom because I knew at that time she wasn't under any desk protecting her. I remember having nightmares about coming home from school only to find that our house had been bombed and my mom was dead. Every time that we had this drill the idea behind it became more real to me. I couldn't imagine life without my mom. Who would take care of us, where would we live, and who would we live with? I didn't want to live with anyone but my mom, except maybe my grandmother. I remember praying to Mary to ask her Son to protect us. The nuns told me that He never says no to His mother, so I became very dedicated to Mary. Prayers were said every hour and as the bell rang we stopped what we were doing and prayed. We prayed for the souls in purgatory and for our family and friends. I would add my own little prayer, asking God to speed the day away.

The intensity of the bullying magnified again when I entered seventh grade. I was feeling pretty bad about my life in general, anyway, then. My dad had left us for another woman, and my mom was beyond sad. I had only one friend that I could relate to, and I felt unaccepted by just about everyone else. A handful of boys were relentless in their pursuit to make my life miserable. A group of boys in particular were the ringleaders; three of them were extremely cruel and two of them were my neighbors. They made sure that the other kids had absolutely nothing to do with me, or else they would pay the same price I was paying. The girls were out to impress the boys, so *no way* would they be seen with me! I attempted to make friends out in the play yard, but the kids just ran away from me saying that I had cooties. No one talked to me, play with me, or was my friend. I quit trying and stayed inside in the lunchroom until it was time to return to class. This was a "no win" situation for me. When I ignored them, they bullied me even more. The few attempts I took to talk back to them failed miserably. They laughed, even, at the way I spoke. They weren't just mean, they were downright cruel; and the glistening I saw in their eyes scared me beyond words. I wanted to die. The pain in my heart and deep in my soul was inconsolable.

During the course of the day we had very structured classes. The first class was religion, of course. The nun called on us randomly and we had to stand at attention while she read the catechism questions, from the homework we'd done, for us to answer publicly. This put a lot of stress on those who didn't study and even for those who did. I always did my homework, partly because I was so obedient and I didn't want to go to hell (or purgatory for that matter); but mostly because I was petrified not to know the answer. I was so anxiety-ridden that I often forgot the answer even if I knew it. This laid me open for more emotional ridicule and taunting from the kids at school. I could hear their snickering, and still I had to stand there and desperately try to remember the answer that I had known perfectly well the night before. So often I wanted to disappear and become invisible. I wanted to have each day pass me by as if it never existed. I think what hurt me the most is that I couldn't understand what I could have done that had made them hate me so. I hardly ever raised my hand in fear of giving the wrong answer and paying the price, not only from the nuns but also from the kids who reminded me of how dumb I was as soon as they had the opportunity to do so.

In several of our subjects we sat according to how "smart" we were. As I look back I wonder what school administrators thought they were achieving by doing this. If it was to shame us into trying harder, they truly failed. It only confirmed what they were telling us: twenty, thirty, or maybe even forty people were smarter than you. My class consisted of fifty children. Math was not one of my strong subjects. I was placed in the second to the last row in math class. I knew I couldn't do math and this proved it. In reading class, however, I sat in the third row there were only four rows. Just the thought of having to get up and change our seats was humiliating in itself. And, once again, the kids had another opportunity to continue their bullying. I can still remember their monkey sounds and snickering. I often wondered why the nuns wouldn't say anything. They had to have known what was happening at least some of the time.

We were not allowed to talk at lunch, in fact our voices could only be heard when we were praying, answering a question, or at recess. As I said, I stopped going out to recess after awhile, knowing no one would play with me but instead would deliberately run away from me. The girls back then had their little cliques. They stayed in their little groups, gossiping, I presume. I could not wait for the day that I would be out of that school and no longer have to deal with a class that would not even look my way except when they were being cruel.

Even my friend Tina could not save me all the time. We were on a different lunch schedule so we never ate lunch together. I felt safer inside. I just ate my lunch really slowly to use up the time. The one and only time I spoke during lunch was when I was in the eighth grade and a younger student was sitting by my side. I offered her my peanut butter sandwich. Big mistake! A nun caught me talking and handed me a blue demerit slip. I started to cry. I couldn't believe I got a demerit slip after so many years of having a clean slate, and—*poof*—with one little sentence it was all taken away. What would my mother think? How would she feel? I didn't want to hurt her. This would hurt her badly. I told the nun how sorry I was and that I just wanted to give this "child" my sandwich. My guardian angel must have touched her soul because she actually took it back. To this day I am thankful to my guardian angel. I knew I would never talk during lunch again.

We had painting on Friday, and everyone seemed to enjoy that. As for me, Friday painting was sort of a release. Surprisingly, we could usually choose whatever we wanted to paint and we had a good portion of the afternoon to do so. I remember we each had our own paint box and paintbrush. If one of the colors cubes in our paint box was nearly empty we had to wait, because we could only get a new one when the cube was completely dry. After we finished our masterpieces we laid our pictures flat on the edge of the windowsills over the weekend to dry. The nun kept our masterpieces in a safe place for the annual art fair. Parents were invited to attend to see the artistic talent of their children.

Friday afternoons always brought promise. The day was about to end and I would finally be released from "prison" and the torture I felt for the weekend. I would then escape to my own little corner of the world, a place where I felt safe—empty, but safe. I counted the minutes in my head and looked forward to retiring to my bedroom.

I lived with the fear that I might go to hell. I knew that hell was a lot easier to get into than heaven. Aside from breathing, everything was a sin. I never understood the place called limbo. I knew it was a peaceful place, with no pain or suffering. All the little babies who never did anything wrong, but died before they were baptized and were deprived of ever seeing God—they went to limbo. It didn't seem fair to me that they had to live in limbo. I couldn't understand: if God were really all just and all fair, how would He allow this, or even make the rule, for that matter? People in purgatory who had sinned had the opportunity to see God, and these poor little babies would never see Him. They never had a chance. Not fair, at all. I was happy that my little sister who died as a baby had been baptized and went straight to heaven.

"Children didn't deserve God," was what one nun told our class. I can remember her saying that she had given up her life for God, and asking what we had done to think that we deserved His glory. I wondered what I could do to be deserving of His love. So I began my difficult journey of trying to gain His love and prove to Him, and the world, that I was not a bad little girl. I did love Him very much, and I could try harder to be good. I already felt I was different and less valuable than all of the fair-skinned kids around me. The kids made sure of that. My French/Italian blood gave me my olive color. I was reminded of how different I was and looked every day, day in and day out. I felt hated, and I was. I even hated myself.

I was in the seventh grade when the kids stated to tell me I was fat. I was always small for my age, but never fat. I had gained some weight over that summer but not really anything to mention, yet they picked up on the weight gain and used it as more ammunition. There was no way out. Or was there? I remember when I was thirteen I asked my mom to buy "Lemon Up" shampoo. It wasn't because I liked the smell or the shampoo, but because I knew that lemon could bleach. I poured it in the bathtub and sat in it in hopes that my skin would lighten so I could be like everyone else. *Why was I cursed with this skin?* I hated myself, and the kids proved to me every day that I was right. I felt *ugly, fat* and *no good*, just as I was called.

At my Catholic school, there was a specific time when we were permitted to go to the bathroom. The only problem with that was my bladder was on a different schedule. I remember one time I was in line to go to the bathroom. I always had to go to the bathroom. This one particular time I had to go so badly that I went to one of the stalls and looked quickly to see if it was taken, rather than to wait my turn. The nun saw me looking and pulled me over to the corner and scolded me. She told me that I was a filthy, dirty, little girl, and God was very displeased with me. I was horrified. *I didn't mean it. I just had to go to the bathroom. I didn't mean to sin! Please, God, forgive me!* This is how I felt. Another time I raised my hand during class, not at the permitted time, to ask the nun if I could go to the bathroom. She ignored me and consequently I ended up going to the bathroom in my chair. This was not the only time I had to go home soaking wet. Fortunately for me, I usually wet myself during the last class of the day, and since it was math class I was at the back of the room. Class ended and I quickly got my coat out of the cloakroom that, luckily for me, was in the back of the room, too. No one noticed. I think they just wanted to get out of school for the day so they didn't pay any attention to me, for a change. I remember how uncomfortable I felt needing to go to the bathroom, but knowing it wasn't going to happen. I remember my eyes swelling up and praying I wouldn't end up going in my underwear because I had to go so badly. It was no use even raising my hand because I would just be ignored. To this very day I still hesitate when I have to excuse myself.

I remember one Friday I came home from school and my mom was cooking beef stew. I told her we could not eat meat on Fridays. She responded that she had forgotten it was Friday, and that it was more of a sin to waste food; God would understand. "No, no," I said. "He would not understand. We will all go to hell." She insisted that it would be okay and got angry with me. It wasn't okay with me, so when she left the kitchen I hid the beef stew underneath my bed. She came back into the kitchen and saw that supper was missing. She knew who was responsible and told me that I had three minutes to put the beef stew back on the counter. I knew she meant it. I did not want to get my mother angrier than she already was. My mother was like the little girl who had a little curl. She was wonderful, but when she lost her temper she later couldn't even remember how she responded to the situation. It wasn't pleasant!

We all sat around the kitchen table and I proceeded to separate the meat from the potatoes and vegetables. I always like separating my food into neat little piles anyway, but I had to do it for that meal. Not one morsel of meat touched my lips. I tried to save the family but I couldn't. However, I saved myself, so I thought. The following Monday at school I confessed to the nuns what had happened. The nun told me that I still shouldn't have eaten the stew because of the beef broth. I felt sick. I had to go to confession and confess my sin and ask for forgiveness. It never happened again. I made sure of that.

Once a month or so our school would have a children's Mass. It was usually a 9:00 AM service. God forbid we forgot to wear a hat or a chapel cap! (A chapel cap was a round piece of lace that sat on top of a person's head). Headwear was required and it was considered a sin if you didn't wear one while attending Mass, or just dropping by for a visit. The children would sit in front with their parents. The nuns sat directly in back of us taking attendance. One particular Sunday as I was on my way out the door of my home, I grabbed *one* red M&M and ate it. Immediately after I ate it, I realized that I would not be able to receive communion, because I couldn't eat or drink for three hours before receiving the body of Christ. I froze. What was I going to do? I remember thinking that if the nuns noticed that I did not go to communion that I would be in big trouble the next day. I already felt that I was a terrible person in their eyes, but if I went to communion, I would be committing a mortal sin. I was nine and did not want to go to hell. What would happen if my mother and I got into a car accident and I died? I would never get to see her. This would be horrible. I hated fire and hell was fire. I wanted to see God some day, and my family, and friends. I felt so confused. I feared the nuns so badly that I decided to risk the perils of hell and go to communion. So I did. I prayed that I would not die before I had the opportunity of going to confession. I told God how sorry I was and that I truly loved Him with all my heart and soul. Luckily for me, we went to confession at school every month. I remember going to confession and confessing my grave sin along with fighting with my sisters, disobeying my mother, telling lies, et cetera. Oh yes, and I kept a chart for the number of times I committed each sin so I wouldn't screw up the amount because then I would have to confess that I lied about how often I'd sinned, too.

I remember on occasion the nuns had a desk check. This was to make sure that our books were in the right order and our pencils were correctly placed in our desks. I always kept a neat desk so I didn't have to worry during desk inspections, which typically happened before lunch and were usually announced. It was after lunch, once day, when a desk check began at random. We had to sit with our hands folded and could not open our desk cover during inspections. The nun approached each one of us and opened our desks for a check. I could not believe my eyes when she opened my desk and found it in disarray. I was shocked and hurt. Someone had played a mean trick on me again. I could hear the snickering. It got worse.

One time I was asked to come to the front of the class and find Africa on the world map. It was right before lunch. I was nervous and scared and I knew I was going to get ridiculed from the kids. As I looked for Africa, I could feel my eyes swell. *Where is it?* I wondered wildly. The nun said, "Well, until Jacquelyn finds Africa we will not go to the lunchroom." She continued as my search went on, "Jacquelyn has just used two minutes of your lunch," and then, "Jacquelyn has used three minutes of your lunch.".... When it got to be five minutes she asked a classmate to point out Africa for me. He saved the day and everyone went to his or her shortened lunch. I paid for that dearly.

As I have said, the kids made fun of the way I talked. I actually spoke as little as I had to and only when I had to. If I smiled they would say that I smiled funny. I remember I was in line waiting to go into the classroom and I smiled about something. During the time that I chose not to communicate I did so only to answer a question, and I often just shook my head as a response. I hated my "baby voice." I remember going home and trying to speak differently, trying not to talk like a baby. I asked myself why I had such a terrible voice. *Why did I have to be so different?* I was so sad, and so depressed, and I didn't know what to do to make myself more acceptable. I felt horrible and could not escape. I felt alone and thought that no one would help me. No one truly understood what I was going through.

I can't even remember what it was but I was probably thinking about going home soon. One of the boys saw me and asked me, "What are you smiling about?" and made a monkey sound. The nun at the time was too busy reprimanding someone else to notice what had just happened. It wasn't often that I even felt like smiling, but this boy took care of that because I stopped smiling completely. They made fun of the way I walked, talked, and smiled. There wasn't anything I could do that was right in their eyes.

Music class was disastrous for everyone. Our teacher asked each of us to stand up individually and sing. Many of the kids couldn't even carry a tune in a bucket, including me, so it was quite embarrassing. The nun often laughed at us. One student was particularly out of tune. I wanted Sister Mary to make the student who was trying to sing stop. He was singing so badly that the class broke out in laughter. I think she enjoyed the whole incident. Humiliation was the name of the game.

Before we graduated from eighth grade the nuns had a talk with the boys and girls about S-E-X. Looking back they never did say the word but they got their point across to us. They affirmed to us that our bodies were temples of the Holy Ghost, period. If that didn't do something to one's conscience then nothing would. How could we even think about that three-letter word? How could we let someone invade our sacred temples? We were also strongly advised not to go on to public high school but to a Catholic high school. I wonder if they ever gave a thought that private schools weren't free and that maybe one could get a solid education by going to a "heathen" school?

My younger sister Debbie who also went to Catholic school tells a story of how, during class one day, she started laughing with her friend Marie. They couldn't stop, even after being reprimanded by the nun. The nun sent the girls out of the classroom and instructed them to get down on their knees and ask Mary the Holy Mother for forgiveness. I believe they stopped laughing after that.

One of the most heart-wrenching times of my life was when one of the students in my class was having a graduation party given by her parents. The kids talked about this party and teased me about not being invited. Evidently it got back to the parents of the girl. One day our doorbell rang and, of course, I ran to answer it. I feared it might be the boy who then always bullied me, threatening my mother with his tomatoes. I answered the door and the girl who was giving the party handed me an envelope. She said, "This is for you," and that was it. She ran back to the car waiting for her, got in, and the car drove off. I opened the envelope, and there was the invitation to the party. I didn't know what to think. I knew for sure that giving me an invitation to her party was not the girl's idea but her parents' plan. I thought about what I should do. I still can't believe I decided to go, but I think it was my determination and my tenaciousness to try to fit in that made me do it. This was my last chance. I couldn't be hurt any more than I had already been, so I had nothing to lose. I also really wanted to see the popular band that her parents had hired. I had hoped that maybe in the end my classmates would reconsider and like me even just a little.

I went to the party reluctantly, but determined enough not to turn back. I sat by myself at a table because no one wanted to get near me. I remember vividly when the band sat down to eat they sat at *my* table. God knows there was room for them to sit elsewhere, and many of the girls looked over at us with envy. I felt good about that until I felt bad about feeling good. I knew I needed help. I felt so lonely and empty inside and felt the deep lump in my throat thicken. I questioned why I had even gone to the party in the first place. I didn't have a good time. I guess in my infinite wisdom I was trying every way I could to be accepted. It never worked out. At that time, the happiest day of my life was leaving that school, knowing that I was going to a new school where no one knew me. I turned this into a celebration of my new life. Maybe I had a chance. I had a chance to begin a new life and find friends. I hung onto the thread and wanted to give life another chance.

At my graduation, I was thrilled that I was finally going to escape. My mom and I went shopping for a pretty graduation dress. Surprisingly enough we did not have to graduate in a uniform. I chose a beautiful, tea-length, blue satin dress. I loved it. My mother told me how beautiful I looked, but I knew she just wanted to make me feel good. I wore my dress to the graduation, and, to my surprise, a girl named Marion (not her real name) had the exact same dress on. Two of my classmates approached me, and with cruelty in their voices, chimed, "That dress looks better on Marion. You look fat in it, and it's wrinkled." It wasn't; but again, I felt devastated. I had loved the dress when my mom bought it for me. I knew I didn't look beautiful in the dress because I wasn't even pretty, but their words were so cruel. Why did they hate me so much? *Why?* I didn't even do anything. I had already stopped smiling but not even that pleased them. I just couldn't win. The best part of the graduation evening was when the ceremony ended and I could leave, *forever.* My family and I went out to dinner.

If I could say *one* positive thing about my experience at Catholic school it would be my interactions with a seventh-grade nun. She was strict, and she was serious, but she could smile. She actually liked me, but she couldn't protect me. I don't think she was aware of what was happening. She was old to me and she reminded me of a grandmother, so in my eyes she did have a few redeeming qualities. I felt okay talking to her and although I could not candidly be open with her, I could approach her after a class. This prevented me from being harassed in the hall. I couldn't share with her what the kids were saying or doing to me because I knew she couldn't do anything to help, and it would make matters worse.

Interestingly, years later, I came in contact with one of my former classmates. I found out from her sister that this classmate had become a doctor and was coming back to Massachusetts for a while. She wanted to know if I would like to see her. My heart sank. Even after all the ensuing years, dreadful memories rushed into my head. She was not one of the bullies, but she, along with the others, had had nothing to do with me. I wasn't sure how I felt about meeting up with her. Maybe, I thought, this would be part of the final healing process for me. I asked her sister if I could contact her. She gave me her e-mail address. I wrote to her and she wrote back, telling me about her own experiences at school.

She told me, to my surprise, how she remembered how terrible and mean *all* the kids were to me. She remembered that I never got in trouble and was very quiet. She told me that she had hated what was happening at school then, and that it had always bothered her and it still bothered her. I started to cry. I could not believe that she felt this way and that my torment had really affected her. I never knew. She had never indicated to me in any way that she liked me. I now understand why. The peer pressure was great and the repercussions were even greater if she had stepped over the line to try to become my friend. She told me she was now a doctor and had always wanted to be a doctor since she was a little girl.

I wrote back to her and I told her that she had never bullied me, and that now as an adult I could understand why she had been compelled to stay with the crowd. She wrote back to me with such gratitude. Our correspondence was a great healer, for both of us. Here is an excerpt from one of her e-mails to me.

> *Hi Jacqui:*
>
> *Your e-mail blew me away. I guess I needed to hear that I wasn't mean to you, I am really glad. Thanks for saying I was just a kid and you now understand about me not standing up to those other kids. I think I was getting traumatized in my own way. All I can say is that I am standing up for others and myself as an adult. I guess I learned a lot from you. I would love to see you again. I am now an OB/GYN. Didn't do pediatrics. I don't like seeing little kids suffer. Hmmm.*
>
> *K.*

I hated every waking moment of my grammar and Catholic school days. I didn't have any fun. Fun was a word in the dictionary but certainly not something for me to experience. I spent all those years trying to better myself in hopes that someday I might be noticed and liked. I felt badly about everything. I hated myself and felt everyone else did, too. It was reinforced time and time again.

I look at all the changes in the Catholic Church that have been made, and oh, how Catholic schools have changed, too! For one, few nuns still teach in Catholic schools. I remember consulting with a priest and asking him if it was still a mortal sin to miss Mass on Sundays and holidays. He said it was not. I searched no further. It is a man-made law anyway. I could never understand why someone who missed church could end up in hell with murderers and rapists. It is no longer a mortal sin to eat meat on Fridays, so what happened to all those people who ate beef stew? We can now receive the host in our hands, walk in a non-Catholic church without fear of the sky falling down, and we can be in our friends' weddings even if they're not Catholic. These are just a few of the changes.

For me, I think it is important to be a good person first. Going to church on Sundays, making novenas, teaching CCD, following the rules of the Church, et cetera, may very well make me a good practicing Catholic but it doesn't necessarily make me a good person. All I had to do was follow the cardinal rule: "Do unto others as you would like done unto you."

I look at the violence in schools today and how kids act out their aggressions. Not all kids are violent before the horrific crimes they commit, but kids who have been bullied, harassed, and tormented by their fellow classmates are often behind such atrocities. They get enraged. Although in no way, shape, or form would I ever condone or justify the horrific acts that do occur, I believe these kids are in enormous pain. I have known that kind of agony.

Through all of my anxieties about sinning, the bullies at school continued to torment me and make me feel sad. I was extremely traumatized by what I endured during my years in Catholic school. I was emotionally hurt and no one cared. I went home and told my mom, and again and again she told me just to ignore them. I finally stopped complaining to her. I was sure everyone was against me, that everyone hated me. Even though a handful of kids verbally took an active roll in the assaults, the entire class ignored me and would not even talk to me. In a way their silence hurt just as much. I didn't think anyone believed me. They thought I was exaggerating. It was only many years later that my thread of hope started to weave itself into the spool it is today.

It was awful—but did I survive Catholic school? Yes, I did!

8

High School

High school was a new beginning for me. I was finally free from the perils of hell. I was free, and determined to make a new start. I no longer had to wear a uniform, when, if my bow was crooked or my blouse was creased, I suffered consequences. I could talk during lunch and hopefully talk freely without being teased or ridiculed. I could talk in the bathroom and that was really okay to do. I no longer had to stand in a line before entering a building and listen to the sounds of bells dictate my moves. I was leaving a school that loved bells. Although this school did have some bells, to me they had a totally different chime. I no longer had to stand still as the first bell rang, or wait to hear the second bell to get in line, and finally the third bell that allowed us to proceed into the building. Was I in heaven? Although there were some rules, they did not compare with those I had left behind at parochial school.

As an initiation to high school, freshman girls were assigned a senior sister, a girl from the senior class who was sort of a mentor. At first I was afraid about who I might get paired with, but when a friend of my sister's, was assigned to me I knew I would be okay. Marianne was very nice. I remember when she and I and my sister (who was also a senior) and her freshman sister went to a local shopping center. We, the freshman girls, had to carry around toilet paper, visible for others to see. I can't remember exactly what we had to do with the paper other than to carry it, but I am sure it wasn't malicious or harmful to others, only embarrassing to ourselves. It was actually fun, and gave me a chance to be silly and careless, which was very foreign to me. I didn't feel that Marianne was ever mean to me and I felt she might even have liked me. We all went out to eat after our shopping center experience—compliments of our senior sisters. I felt good being with my two "sisters." What a difference. Was I on the same planet? I could have cried—joyfully, of course. From the initiation with Marianne, I knew, with my usual reservation, that if I had a problem or concern I had someone to whom I could turn. Imagine: a senior in high school was my *friend*, how lucky was that? I had my real sister around during her last year of high school, too, so I also had her great support I had a good year ahead of me to adjust to my new environment. Most of my former classmates from the Catholic grammar school went on to a Catholic high school, and even if they had also chosen the same high school I attended we didn't cross each other's path that often. The high school was large. I chose to be in the business course section of the high school that consisted of courses such as typing, and bookkeeping, and such. Most others chose the general or the college course path, making even more of a gulf between the mean kids and me.

I still felt very shy and not quite sure about how I would be accepted. I remained very reserved throughout my four years in high school, but I learned a lot and I grew a lot. I vowed to be somebody and make something out of my life. I would prove to the world that I wasn't as bad and as ugly as I thought the mean kids saw me. I met and became friends with a girl Linda, a girl named Doreen, and another girl named Barbara. We never became very close; but they were school friends, and I was happy to have them. I kept my distance, but at least I had friends who actually liked me. This was wonderful. It was a good start to my new beginning.

I remember the first semester as a freshman in particular detail. I was in math class and a girl passed a note to me. *This is for me?* I thought. *Wow! She is actually passing a note to me!* I took the note and read it. She asked me in the note if I had seen *Dr. Kildare* the night before. We had talked about how cute and handsome he was. I proceeded to write back that he was, indeed, a hunk. As I handed it back to her the teacher caught me in the act. Oh my God! I could not believe that for the very first thing I did I got caught! Would I get a demerit? For a moment I thought I was back in Catholic school.

The teacher asked me, "Jacqui, would you like to read that to the class?"

"No," I answered, awaiting his larger reaction.

Someone up there liked me that day because the teacher only said, "Okay, I hope this won't happen again." I assured him it would not.

It never did happen again. I learned my lesson. Although it wasn't Catholic school, this school had rules, too.

Oh well, nice try, I thought. I was still somewhat thrilled because it had been kind of fun doing something mischievous. It was a new experience for me. Many would probably laugh off this little incident as nothing special, but for me it was a giant step towards releasing myself of the fear to take a chance.

I never felt like I totally belonged throughout high school, but at least I didn't mind going to school *as much* as I had in the past. I didn't participate much in any activities because I was too shy and didn't feel I was good at anything, anyway. I never wanted to get involved with anything or anyone because I feared the rejection that I felt would surely follow. I felt that I would rather have them wonder who I was than discard me. I never went to a prom or dance or did any of the other fun activities that teenagers do. I felt different. I felt that all the girls were pretty, and I wasn't. Every girl looked thinner than me. As I walked down the halls I still wanted to be invisible. In my mind, I was still a broken sparrow. I didn't want to feel that way but I didn't know how to get rid of the pain and the emptiness I felt deep inside me.

I never had gym in Catholic school so it was a new experience for me. I never had actually participated in any sports, so I was totally unfamiliar with any of the sport activities. It didn't take me long to discover that I was not very good at the sports that were required for us during gym. I soon despised gym. I felt very uncoordinated and doing something that made me act clumsily was all I needed to add to my fears. I was a terrible teammate. I watched the volleyball come toward me and protected myself from getting hit rather than to hit it to a teammate or over the net. I could understand why I wasn't really welcomed on any team. I was used to rejection, though, so I numbed myself to any adverse reactions.

For a while, I knew a competitive game with the opposing team was coming up in gym, and I worried about how I would survive the class period. I couldn't bear the embarrassment of letting down my team members. I actually lost sleep with anxiety. I decided that the only solution was not to go at all. I would just skip gym class. Yes, I was going to do it. I had a plan.

After I finished my lunch I walked down to the guidance office and admitted my offense. I told the counselor that I was skipping my gym class. I told her I was there to turn myself in. Her first response to me was, "Who are you, my dear?" Obviously, I wasn't a frequent visitor to the principal's office. I imagined that she was quite surprised by my actions. But, I think part of me felt guilty and part of me feared getting caught if I didn't admit to my crime. I was allowed to stay in the office and read until my next class.

During the sixties short dresses were in. The shorter the better; that was the style. I remember how wonderful it was shopping for school clothes and how much fun I had. I no longer had to wear a uniform and I could choose a wardrobe for the first time ever. I wore size 7/8 (although I still felt fat) so I had many choices from which to choose. I remember one time the gym teacher made all the girls kneel on the floor and if the hem of their dress did not touch the floor, they were sent to the principal's office for detention. This is one time I was glad I had short legs. It was close, but I was saved.

I never dated in high school, never went to any dances, and never participated in any extra-curricular activities. I actually did get asked to go to the junior prom with a young man. I couldn't say yes. I thought it was a big joke, and he didn't really mean it by asking me. Metaphorically, I've always let people up to my door, but I've never allowed them to step inside and really get to know me. That would have been too big of a risk for me then. I was an empty shell.

During my senior year I read an advertisement posted in one of my business classes looking for students to do store inventory for one day during the month of January. I called the number printed on the ad and was told that I could report to the local department store. They were going out of business and needed to move out. I remember the day I worked was a Sunday and there were five of us working together. It was a very labor-intensive job that consisted of counting merchandise, taking it off the shelves, packing it in boxes, and stacking it in a corner to be loaded on a truck. The man in charge was a very demanding, demeaning person. It was clear from the start that he did not like me. He knew my name was Jacqui but insisted on calling me Blackie. This hurt me deeply, but I didn't feel like I had the right to say anything to him. I worked like a dog without a break. I noticed the other four workers taking time out and lazing off a bit. Later, they all took a break for supper, and he let them go, one by one. Did they just take it upon themselves to take a break or did he actually give them permission? I will never know, but I did know that I did not feel justified in taking the liberty to leave my station. I waited for him to tell me to take a break instead. He never did. As I grew tired and hungry I wondered when it would be my turn to have a break and relax. I did ask permission to go to the bathroom but I felt I had to rush back to continue working.

He never once called me by my correct name, but only by the name Blackie. I remember crying inside but being determined not to let it show outside. The words of the kids who bullied me kept echoing in my head reminding me of how "bad" it was to be olive skinned. I felt this is what he wanted. I couldn't wait for the day to end. The day finally ended at 10:00 PM. I was exhausted and hungry and couldn't wait to get home and share my experience with my mom. I felt afraid, because he was an adult who had venom in his veins, and I felt helpless to do anything about it. It was part of one of my high school experiences that left a mark. As I had done all my life, I forced myself into doing things that should have been fun but I couldn't seem to have a good time. I always felt that I had to watch myself for anything I might say or do. I didn't want to appear stupid or look awkward or out of place. This was my fear, what I felt inside, and what haunted me.

"Senior Week" came, five days full of fun and interesting activities. It was the final farewell to high school life. I didn't attend many of the festivities; however, I did attend my senior banquet with my school friend Doreen. I remember thinking how nice it was to have a friend who really liked being with me, but I still kept in mind that she might not like me for much longer. We were just school friends. We didn't see each other outside of the school walls except for the two functions that I attended during senior year. The other activity aside from senior banquet was the senior picnic held at a well-known beach on the North Shore. I am glad that I chose to go because I have good memories from them in my memory bank.

My senior year was the best year of my entire school life, only because it was the last year. I was going to graduate, and I set my sights on just that. I would soon have the chance and the freedom to do what I wanted to do. It was my life, and I could choose the road this time. Each day was one day closer to graduation. I carefully checked off each day and thanked God for helping me make it through to the end. I graduated on June 6, 1968. I couldn't believe that I had finally made it. I wasn't sure what my next step of action was going to be, but I didn't care. This was enough action for me. It was a bittersweet day, unfortunately. On this same day, Senator Robert Kennedy was assassinated. We all said a prayer for him and his grief-stricken family. As I received my diploma, I remember thinking, *Jacqui, you made it. The sky is the limit.* This was going to be the first day of the rest of my life. I was free.

Looking back on those days I think to myself what I would have done different. Well, hindsight is 20/20, so needless to say I would have done everything different. If I knew then what I know now, I would have been in control and not have allowed others to control me. I would have laughed, sang, and enjoyed more of what life had to offer. I would probably still have a difficult time understanding why I was treated the way I had been treated and why others acted the way they did. However, I hope that I would have been able to stand up for myself. I know I would have.

Jacqui's High School Graduation June 6, 1968

9

Modeling

To this day I don't know how I mustered up enough confidence to enroll in modeling school. Perhaps I was still out to prove that I existed, and that I was someone who had something to say and something to offer the world. I had always envied the models that I saw as I thumbed through glamour magazines. The women featured were all so beautiful. They were all so thin. They were blessed with such beauty. They looked so happy, and I felt they were so lucky. They had so much confidence. They seemed to have it all. I wanted to be part of that. I had a dream, and I wanted it to come true. I wanted to be noticed in a positive way, not in the negative way that I saw myself and felt others saw me. I hung onto the thread of hope that somehow I could have *one* thing that I wanted. Why did it seem to me that everyone else's dreams came true?

In one of the magazines that I happened to be reading one afternoon was an advertisement for a school located in Boston that offered a program in modeling. It guaranteed a professional portfolio and leads to the best modeling jobs. It caught my attention. I was then about to graduate from high school and had no immediate plans. I knew I wouldn't be going to college. I wasn't sure what I was capable of accomplishing, but I knew I had to do something because I felt lost. College was for a smart person so I knew that wasn't the answer, and I didn't want to work in retail. I had to decide what to do with my life. This seemed like the perfect plan. It seemed adventurous to me.

I guess I would have to attribute my decision to move ahead with this plan partly to my own tenaciousness and drive. I had an innate desire to help myself feel better about me. Underneath the deep-rooted scars was the little girl who at age three had sung songs in front of relatives and danced to the Mexican Hat dance. I felt robbed of that part of my personality. It had been torn from me at a very early age and I wanted it back. My life seemed to take on an entirely different course than it would have if things continued as they began. Life is full of twists and turns, as I found out.

I applied to the school and shortly afterward received a letter in the mail to set up an appointment for an interview. I was so excited. I got accepted! At the same time, my sister Jeanne was interested in fashion merchandising. They also offered this program at the school, and she too got accepted. She was excited to begin her own new endeavor. She hated her job and was looking for a new start. This made it perfect for both of us because we could travel together.

This could be a new beginning for me. I just might become famous—*ha-ha*! Anyway, it was worth it to me. I would continue working part-time, pay for my tuition, and hope that I could land a modeling career. I was determined to free myself of my negative thoughts and the way I felt about myself. I was determined to try anything I could to be someone and to feel better about myself. Many years later I learned that I always looked in the wrong places for help. I never looked inside my heart and soul. Perhaps it was too painful. But then, I told myself I was going to be somebody, *just you wait and see*. I continued on my never-ending diet that I had been on since eighth grade and this new adventure gave me more of an incentive to continue than ever before.

I began my journey into the modeling world in September of 1968. There was an enormous amount of competition. I enjoyed the trip into the big city of Boston. My sister and I drove in together through the traffic, over the Mystic River Bridge, onto Storrow Drive, and made our way into downtown Boston. A full day of classes included fencing, runway walking techniques, makeup application, hair care, and how to market oneself. I enjoyed it all. I made a new friend named Barbara. We connected from the start, and I felt so good inside to have someone who wanted to be my friend. We remain dear friends today.

It wasn't all fun, though. One of my teachers must have been a tormented individual because she seemed to enjoy making others feel horrible. She humiliated and criticized students in front of other students. I wanted the school to be an entirely positive experience, but this teacher brought back horrible memories for me. I still felt pretty bad about myself so it didn't take much for me to feel hurt. She didn't have to try hard. I believe it came natural to her.

I remember one time we had dance class, and I had to go to the bathroom. Now, most people would just excuse themselves and go to the bathroom, right? Not me. Memories of Catholic school still enveloped me. The fear I felt stopped me from just leaving the room. Unfortunately, I ended up going to the bathroom on the floor. I was totally embarrassed and soaked through, to say the least. I ended up crying, feeling fully humiliated. I remember I was in the back of the room, and this had happened toward the end of the class period. When class was over the students exited toward the front door. I exited through the back door. I went into the bathroom and cleaned myself up the best I could. I got paper towels and proceeded to wipe up the floor before my secret was exposed. My good friend Barbara was in the same dance class, and she stood by me and helped me through this terrible experience.

Another time I was in a fashion show at the school. Parents, friends, and relatives were invited to attend. It gave us an opportunity to show off what we had learned and how well we could model. It was also a contest to pick the Model of the Month. I was truly enthused by this. I came in second! I couldn't believe it. Me! I was so thrilled. But my high was about to become another low period in my life.

Afterward, I was in the ladies room and the teacher who had been so nasty before approached me. She told me that my hair looked dirty and it was unkempt. It wasn't. I had just washed it and had it nicely styled. I remember breaking down in front of her and crying. For once in my life I had begun to feel positive, at least a little. She never comforted me nor did she say she was sorry. She just walked away leaving me alone, crying. I regained my composure and went back to the small reception they were having after the show to join my mom and sister. They never knew what had happened. All I remember is them saying how wonderful I did and that helped to ease the pain.

When I had my portfolio pictures taken I asked a member of the faculty if he would be so kind as to pose with me for one of my pictures. To my surprise, he agreed. I was thrilled. His name was Charles L., and he had actually played a small part in a movie with Jack Lemmon titled *The Out-of-Towners*. How lucky could one be? I got to pose with a real-life movie star. I couldn't help but think, *How do you like me now?* This is what I thought, but not what I felt. I couldn't believe that this "movie actor" actually agreed to have his picture taken with me. *Me?* All who looked at my pictures would see me with him. How exciting this was for me. I can still remember the thrill I had held inside my heart, but after all that attention why did I still feel worthless? Why did I still feel it wasn't real? I wasn't sure what was in store for me or where all this was leading, but I knew that I was going to enjoy this dream for a while. I knew it wouldn't last but I could at least smile and make-believe that everything was now okay.

After I graduated from the modeling school I met with a professional photographer to take pictures for my portfolio. He took several pictures of me in different poses and settings. We went to Back Bay in Boston and the Boston Common amongst other areas for the photo shoots. I remember what a wonderful experience this was. We shot a few pictures in a professional studio where I posed for several "character" shots, wherein one poses as a particular character, such as a secretary, a dancer, a chef, et cetera. These pictures were to be presented to different modeling jobs for which I was applying.

I remember making an appointment to meet with a modeling agent to discuss my career. I didn't know what I was in for, but the whole idea of meeting with a true-blue agent excited me. I knew the career of modeling was very competitive and I didn't feel confident, but I hoped to build that confidence. I wanted to succeed and I wanted to feel like I was someone. The pain was still great. I was still so naïve. I played the part and acted bravely as I entered the room where I was about to meet a person who might be the answer to a successful modeling career. I had nothing to lose. I was anxious and excited for my interview. It was scary to me, but also I felt it would be very adventurous. It was, and proved to be very different than I had expected.

I remember the day of the meeting with the modeling agent. I walked into his office, sat down and this is what transpired.

The agent greeted me and invited me to have a seat. He informed me that he was going to ask me a few questions that I needed to answer to give him a better perspective of what I was actually looking for in a modeling career.

After a few initial questions, he began.

"Jacqui, how far would you go for a good modeling job?"

After a considerable amount of time to think over a good answer I said, "New York?"

I remember the look on his face. It was a look of disbelief. *Are you for real? Are you serious?* It felt like forever, but I knew I didn't give him the answer he was looking for. Should I have said California?

"No, that is not what I meant."

I was so embarrassed. I thought through my answer carefully this time and proceeded to tell him, "I would probably agree to model underwear."

Oh, no, I said to myself, *I guess I did it again. The answer was wrong, wrong. Please God, help me with this quiz! Oh well, I give up.* Like I said, I was Ms. Naïve.

"Modeling is very competitive and sometimes you have to compromise. Are you willing or able to do that?"

"No," I heard myself answer.

I think he knew that I would probably have a tough time making it in modeling. I am sure he suspected my career would be short lived.

Models work darn hard and practice many hours to "perfect their style." There is a lot of competition and it can often be really tough. I am only sharing my own personal experience. I think the agent was being blunt with me, which was a good thing because knowing myself as I did, I knew I would probably compromise very little even if it were as simple as modeling underwear.

I managed to land a few good jobs. I did several runway-modeling jobs, some of which were at shopping malls. I landed another modeling job at a local supper club on the North Shore where I lived. There, I visited patron's tables and modeled the latest fashions with style and grace. It was interesting to meet the types of ladies and gentlemen who went out for leisurely lunches. I helped promote the opening of a local business and I continued to reach for the stars in hopes of a lucrative career. I needed a job that had security, though. I needed a job that guaranteed me a salary each and every week. However, my jobs weren't pulling in enough income for me to survive, but I enjoyed modeling for as long as it lasted.

I really enjoyed this experience. I remember thinking, "if only those mean and nasty kids could see me now." Although I still didn't feel pretty and my insecurities still lurked deep inside, I was happy that I had taken on this adventure. I had locked my insecurities deep inside of me and went forward.

Although I never became a top model I still totally enjoyed the experience. I am not sorry for one moment that I chose modeling as one of my journeys in life. I would do it again. It was fun and exciting. I met my movie star and my wonderful friend Barbara, and had a great opportunity to grow.

My need for helping people less fortunate than myself still urged me to move forward. This led me to obtain a position at the local state school for children with developmental disabilities. This was a very positive next step and one that I never regretted.

10

Adam

I was nineteen years old when I met Adam, who was then twenty-three. I couldn't believe that I was actually dating a twenty-three-year-old man. He really liked me. I was introduced to him at a New Year's Eve party that my older sister was giving for her friends. I was lucky enough to be invited. I couldn't believe that at the end of the evening he asked me if he could call me sometime. He said that he wanted to take me out. I was so happy to give him my phone number.

Adam was my first love. I felt like I was walking on water with him. I felt euphoric. He was handsome, smart, and had a great personality. He was a drafts-man by trade. He made me feel special. He made me smile. I remember waiting at night for him to call and I also remember my mom saying that I should never wait for a guy to call because they can always call back. Forget that I thought. He called me the following week on a Wednesday. I remember it was a Wednesday because I had been counting the days until I heard from him. I remember feeling on the top of the world when he asked me out. I couldn't believe my ears. I had never thought he would actually call me.

For our first date, we went out for a nice, relaxing dinner and for a drive along the shore. I was so happy. We only dated five short months, but I will never forget him. It took me a very, very long time to get over him and I blamed myself for our breakup. I wondered why he had liked me in the first place. I was very naïve to the ways of the world and, of course, he was quite the opposite. My curfew was 12:00 AM then, and I never would have entertained the thought of returning home even one minute past that time. My mom still had so many restrictions on me, and I felt sure he had never encountered a date like me before. I felt torn as usual. I did not want to hurt my mother, I was very obedient, and I didn't want to get her angry with me; however, I felt resentment for the way I felt. I was so rigid but I could not release myself from within the invisible restraints I imprisoned myself.

One evening, Adam had taken me dinner and a movie in Boston, and I remember I felt so beautiful. This was a rare feeling for me. I had such a wonderful time that night. I was with someone who made me feel sensational. I was in the big city feeling so secure. I wanted the evening to last forever. I felt as though I were having a beautiful dream and I never wanted to awaken. However, I also felt as Cinderella must have felt the night she went to the prom. I didn't want the evening to end but I knew at 12:00 AM I had to be back home. I remember looking at my watch as we left the movie, which, to my horror read 11:30 PM. My fear and concern was how we were ever going to make it home for 12:00 AM? You know what? We did. Adam knew how I felt and he knew the rules in my home were not to be broken. I felt so bad for Adam. All the way home I kept thinking how he probably never had a girlfriend like me, especially one that had a curfew. I remember the ride home was tense. Adam didn't seem to mind, at least on the outside, but I think I was upset for both of us. We arrived in my driveway at 11:59 PM. My heart was beating fast. I was so anxious. I thought he must have been thinking, *This is ridiculous.* Would he ever call me again? I was so nervous that I was sick to my stomach. I thought he must have been wondering why he ever asked me out. I wondered that, too. We hardly had time for a goodnight kiss.

To my surprise, Adam did call me again. I was so happy that he still cared, and in fact that he respected that I had to be home no matter what. Another evening, after Adam and I had been out to dinner, we sat in the parking lot of the restaurant and talked awhile. He slowly moved over and put his arm around me. I knew he wanted to kiss me. As we were kissing and truly enjoying our warm kisses, I heard "sounds of excitement." The words of the nun's conversation from so very long ago echoed in my head. "It's a sin to get boys excited." His advancements made me nervous. Why couldn't I enjoy this? What did "excited," mean, anyway? I didn't even know. I just knew it wasn't "right." That is what I was told. I knew that I had to push him away. *It's a sin, a horrible sin to get them excited.* I was so brainwashed that everything was sinful. I believed that whatever was happening was my fault and I had caused this terrible thing. But what could be so terrible about it?

I was angry and frustrated because I believed that even a good night kiss could lead me to the "pathways of destruction." Adam pulled away and sat back into the seat, and I thought that for sure this would be the end of our relationship. I wanted to continue kissing him. It had felt good. He certainly liked it, too. What was wrong with that? Why did I have to be so strict and feel so guilty about *everything*! I was determined to try to rid myself of these feelings and be more relaxed to see if I could allow myself a little more freedom from my self-imposed imprisonment. Although there were no bars on my personal prison, the invisible ones might have just as well been impenetrable bars of steel.

We celebrated Christmas together by exchanging gifts. I remember Adam gave me a bottle of Estee Lauder perfume. It smelled so nice and I was flattered that he had bought me such a lovely gift. I, in exchange, bought him an engraved pewter mug with his initials that I had found at an exquisite jewelry store called Daniel Lowe's. We kissed each other and again I had a feeling like I had never felt before. I never wanted my time with Adam to end. I believed I was falling in love. Could I be so lucky? Could I actually build up a trust in someone? It was too early to think about that.

One evening Adam and I went to a party at his friend's house. It started out as a wonderful party and I was having a great time. I mingled with the group, feeling a bit of confidence about being accepted by them. I was with his friends and they all loved him so I felt I had a great edge. Unfortunately, one of the guests loved Adam a little bit too much. As I found my way back to Adam after a short while, I was shocked and hurt, and I could not believe my eyes. Adam and another woman were making out in a corner. They were so involved that they did not even realize at first that I was there watching them. I felt sick to my stomach. When they pulled themselves out of their trance Adam noticed that I was in the room, noticeably shaking. He approached me and walked me outside to the connecting porch. He held me in his arms tightly as if he could stop my shaking. "I am so sorry," he said. He told me that the woman was a former girlfriend and he hadn't seen her for a long time. He told me that he still cared about her deeply. He also told me he never meant to hurt me. He continued to express his sorrow and regret, and said that whoever got me would be the luckiest person in the world.

Somehow none of what Adam said helped me feel better. *He could have me*, I thought, *if he really wanted me*. I wanted another chance to prove my love. I just needed time. I was afraid. I knew I was going to lose him to this "new" found, old love. I got the feeling that he was saying good-bye to me then. I didn't want to believe it, but deep within my heart and soul I knew it was true. He stayed with me the rest of the evening, but, if I remember correctly, we did leave early. I think he felt uncomfortable and I was tense. I don't know to this day if he went back to the party after he dropped me off at home, but my guess is that he did. I lay in bed that night and thought how if I hadn't been so afraid, guilty, and confused about what was right and wrong I would still be in his arms. Why couldn't I loosen up just a little? I hated myself, but what else was new?

I didn't know what would happen next. I decided that I was going to wait for him to call. *Surely he would at least call me, wouldn't he?* I wanted so badly to tell him that I would try to change. I wanted a chance to explain my confusion to him. I loved him and I couldn't lose him. In my heart I believed that a life with Adam was too good to last and I knew that it was only a matter of time before I would have lost him anyway. At the same time I had hoped I was wrong. I still hung on to the thread of hope. He did call, incredibly, and he asked me out again.

Adam and I did continue to see each other for a short time after that incident. I believe he decided to see me because he felt badly and maybe a little guilty for hurting me so blatantly. But, again, maybe not; maybe he wanted to give it one more try. I will never know his motives, but it doesn't matter now. I was on my best behavior. I tried to be more open and I really tried to understand him and be more receptive and caring. I didn't want him to go away. I had finally found a little happiness in my life. I would like to feel that I did the same for him.

One day he just stopped calling. I never got an explanation. He just didn't call anymore. I gave myself every excuse why he wasn't calling. I waited by the phone night after night, week after week, and month after month, until I finally came to the realization that he wasn't going to call. Then, one evening the phone rang and it was Adam. I couldn't believe my ears. I was very cautious not to say the wrong thing. He was very nice but very different, cool and collected. I knew he was saying goodbye and that he finally mustered up the courage to call me. I loved hearing his voice and didn't want the conversation to end. I hoped and prayed that he would ask me out just one more time. He never said he would or would not call me again, and I was afraid to ask him. He never did call again. I cried every day until there were no tears left. I knew I would never find another man like him. I don't think he ever realized how much I truly cared for and loved him, nor do I think he ever realized how much I appreciated what he gave me. He helped weave the thread of hope I had always held on to, and he helped me begin to sense that I could be liked or even loved.

I often think of Adam and would love to know how he is. I bet he has a beautiful wife and family now because he was truly a beautiful man. I never got that same feeling back again. It was a gift.

11

Brian

It was December 1970 when my brother-in-law John came home for a short leave from the service. He was stationed at Fort Dix in New Jersey. He was engaged to my sister Jeanne and they were to be married the following February. It was a long drive from New Jersey so he brought along a friend. His name was Brian.

It was a snowy wintry day when they arrived at our home. As Brian walked in the door our eyes met and we knew there was a connection instantly. He had big blue eyes, blond hair, and the most beautiful "peaches and cream" complexion I had ever seen. He was a dream. And, he was actually attracted to me. We spent a wonderful weekend together, and by the end of it I was cautiously optimistic. I imagined it would be only a matter of time before he didn't care for me but I wanted to give it a chance. I was so afraid and no one truly understood how badly I felt about myself. I had so wished that I could have been blond with light skin and light-colored hair like Brian. I believed that if I had been born with those features I would have been so happy with my life because I would have been automatically accepted by society. I lived with these thoughts constantly.

Once the weekend visit was over I was sure I would never see him again. *Wrong.* He wanted to see me again! Wow! Could it be true? He asked me if he could write to me when he got back to the base. *Yes, I would love to hear from you.* He wanted to write to me *and* he wanted to see me again. I thought I must have been dreaming. *Does he really like me?* I felt warmth, love, kindness, and a need for him. This was my chance, another opportunity to have someone to love and to love me in return. I knew that given the chance, I could show him that I am a good person. I would be so good to him. I would never hurt him. I wanted the opportunity, but of course I was afraid, too, that he would soon reject me. I was going to try to be more relaxed, more open to his warmth, and try to get closer and not feel so guilty even with a kiss.

Brian and I wrote to each other all the time. He made it a point to come up to Massachusetts with John whenever he had the opportunity to do so. I sent him postcards, care packages, and letters. It was so much fun doing this. I had my own guy to write to until we could be together again. I had heard other girls talk about their own special guy and how they were anxiously waiting their return, and I had envied them. I had felt that I would never be one of those lucky people, but I was wrong and darn glad that I was. I now had my own guy who I could talk to, write letters to, and, best of all, spend time with. We talked for hours on end, sharing our life experiences.

We were very young then, although I didn't feel that young at the time. I felt quite ready for a relationship and was determined to make one with Brian work. I wanted to trust and I wanted to be able to love him completely. I wanted to rid myself of all the negative feelings and thoughts that clouded my mind and kept me from being whole. I wanted to share my life story with him and I wanted to know about his life. I cared about him and was most interested to learn more. He mattered to me, and he cared about me.

I told him mainly about what I did rather than who I was. I felt this was a safer route. At the time, I was working at a school for developmentally disabled children where I cared for them and taught them daily living skills. I loved the kids and I felt good about being able to help them. I brought Brian to the school where I worked to meet my kids and he too fell in love with them. I loved him for that. He helped me bring one of the children home one day to celebrate the child's birthday. His name was Percy and he was turning eleven years old chronologically, but mentally he was about nine months.

Brian told me he came from a small town in the Midwest. He had lived on a farm and he missed his family very much. He also told me that his parents were divorced and that he had a brother. He had stayed with his mom when his brother went with his dad. He said the only thing he could remember from his parents' split was his mom packing his brother's clothes. *How sad is that*, I thought. My heart went out to him. I couldn't imagine being separated from my siblings. We were so close and that is how we survived our traumas. I felt a deep sadness of how horrible that must have been. He was special, I saw, and I wanted to take away any pain he might have.

I wanted to learn just who Brian was. I cared, and wanted him to know how interested I was in him. He acquiesced, telling me that he was a beekeeper and explained to me all I wanted to know about keeping bees. He told me that high school graduating class consisted of thirty-two students and that half of the graduating students were his cousins. Now that is something for the books. I could hardly believe that a town could be so small. I lived in a small town myself but there was no comparison with where he grew up and lived. I later learned that it was as unique as I thought.

Onc Sunday I asked Brian if he would like to attend Mass with me. He said he would and so we went to church together. I remember feeling happy that he agreed to go with me. I thought this was pretty nice of him considering he wasn't even Catholic. He was interested in *my* life, too. He was very open and wanted to get involved with my interests. This made me love Brian even more. I took him all around the North Shore area of Massachusetts. He loved the ocean so I brought him to see the great beaches we had, including Good Harbor Beach in Gloucester, Massachusetts. The beach's enormous waves crashed against the rocks with fury. The water never got quite warm enough for a comfortable swim but if you were adventurous enough you could try a "cool" dip in the ocean. I also took him to see the infamous Witch House in Salem, Massachusetts, and the House of Seven Gables, which is a great tourist attraction. He found all of these sights exciting and I so enjoyed taking him to see this part of the country that he had never seen. Also, I had lived in this part of the country all my life and had never before taken the opportunity to explore it myself.

Brian was warm, sensitive, loving, caring, and everything I dreamed a man could be. He loved my brother John like his own brother and actually seemed to take a special interest in him. Maybe he was missing his own brother. He played ball with Johnny and formed a close relationship with him. I was so happy about this because my brother never really had a male figure around and he desperately needed one. He loved Brian and Brian loved Johnny. He fit into our family perfectly, and I just loved that. My mother loved him, too, and kind of took him under her wing. He loved her cooking and he enjoyed everything she prepared.

Every time Brian had to go back to Fort Dix I could not stop thinking about him. I would lie in bed missing his sweet lips and soft touch and his special kindnesses to me. I still could not believe that he loved me. I was still afraid that if I allowed myself to be vulnerable I would lose control and be hurt.

One weekend Brian came down from New Jersey alone. He had some leave time and he wanted to see me. We spent the weekend enjoying each other's company and talking about our lives. We were forming a bond. We got into some very personal issues and he told me how he had once been engaged to a woman named "Mattie." On a leave from the service he flew home to visit her. She told him she had met someone else and she was going to marry that person. This news devastated him. I did not want to ask him too many questions about it because I could see the pain in his face. I felt he still had strong feelings for her and he hadn't really gotten over her. This concerned me.

I felt so badly for him. I knew I could never do that to him. I loved him and I knew he loved me. I wondered, though, whether ours was a rebound relationship or if it was for real. It felt real; at least I wanted it to be real. The trust issue that I always struggled with hit me hard. Why couldn't I trust completely? I knew why, but I didn't want to face my self-doubt. Would I remain single forever? Could I accept this? Did I even want to get married or just want-to-want? Was I making a big deal out of nothing? I tried to ignore my inner feelings. I hated myself for not being able to fight my insecurities but I was determined to try.

In February Jeanne married John and moved to New Jersey. I flew down to visit her, and, of course, my love, Brian. It was the first time he used the words "I love you." Our love continued to grow stronger but for me doubts always hung over my head. I still had a long way to go and it was a daily struggle to make it right. I wanted the doubts to disappear. I wanted to escape the "monsters" within me. We continued to date, enjoying each other's company. I flew to New Jersey and he flew to Massachusetts. I felt Brian was getting ready to pop the big question. He would soon be getting out of the service and he had to decide what he was going to do. Was he returning home without me or staying in Massachusetts? Brian decided to stay.

On May 1, 1971, Brian asked me to marry him. He wanted to give me a ring. I didn't know what to say. I *still* couldn't believe that I had a boyfriend who enjoyed being with me, never mind the thought of him wanting to marry me. I wondered if by saying yes I was making the right decision. I wasn't sure. It hadn't been that long that we had dated, but how could I say no to such a wonderful person who loved me? This frightened me. I wanted to be sure, but I knew needed more time. I didn't want to lose Brian, but I also wasn't sure of what I really wanted. I couldn't say, "I love you" at that moment, but I hoped somehow he knew I did. I needed more time, and "I love you" was such a commitment. Although I felt I loved him, I wasn't sure and doubted I never would be.

I knew what it meant to be married, at least in my eyes, and that frightened me. Doubts filled my mind and heart. If I said I loved him, I felt committed. I couldn't commit. I wasn't ready for the rejection that I knew would probably come. I was totally confused. I thought about what I should do and with some hesitation I said yes. I remember thinking, *Wow, I am getting engaged.* It was surreal to me and it didn't feel as good as I thought it would, but how could it with all of my confusion? On the other hand, I never ever thought this would happen to me. I knew I had a lot of work to do. I had a wonderful guy who loved me, treated me like an angel, and was a totally respectable man. I knew I could pray to God to help me rid myself of all the doubts I had, not about Brian, but about marriage. So, after that soul searching I was ready for the next big step. I needed time and I knew it was up to me. I didn't want anything to stand in our way; however, it was me who was the biggest obstacle. I was afraid.

Brian and I went shopping for rings. We went to a store in the town where I lived and we picked out a beautiful solitaire diamond. I remember going back to my house and finding no one at home. He took out the ring and as he put it on my finger he whispered in my ear, "I love you, Mattie!" Did I hear *Mattie*? My heart skipped a beat, maybe two beats. Could I have heard it wrong? I didn't want to believe my ears, but my ears rang true. He did say Mattie. Was this a sign? Was I listening to what God might have been telling me? I probably would have thought I heard wrong, but what he said afterwards confirmed it. Brian apologized to me for calling me his former girlfriend's name. I was devastated. I was getting engaged, and he was calling me by another woman's name. I tried to make light of it. I *knew* he loved me and I was going to fight the feeling of foreboding I had. As it was I was already fighting my own obstacles that were getting in my way. I wanted to believe it was an honest mistake, but it was hard to understand how or why this mistake had to happen at such an important time in our lives. I blamed myself because of my own insecurities. I tried to convince myself that this was my chance to have a great life with someone who loved me, and a chance to have a family of my own. I would probably never have the chance again. I decided to try to work it out inside my soul and hoped that I would have enough time before Brian got tired of waiting for me. I felt, though, like I was pushing a river and I knew it shouldn't be as difficult as that.

Brian was beautiful inside and out and I didn't want to let him go. I knew that becoming engaged had been to make a total commitment to Brian. It meant a promise to share my life with him forever and ever, through thick and thin, happiness and sadness. Was I sure Brian was the right person for me, or would anybody be, for that matter? Why did I have so many doubts about myself? Was I too young to know at twenty years old? Could I bear to live so far away from home? Would Brian want to move back to the Midwest? I knew he had a job waiting for him at home. I was so close to my family that this idea terrified me. I was consumed by all these questions and thoughts. It just didn't feel right. It should have been, I felt, a time of feeling on top of the world, free of worries, a feeling that one could conquer anything. I felt far from this. I wanted it to feel right but the more I forced it the more it eluded me. I was so angry with myself, but again I convinced myself that I was going to give it a try and not give up. I wanted to be fair to Brian and also give myself a chance to chase out the demons that seemed always to lurk around any relationship that came my way. Was there any hope, even a thread?

Brian was released from the service in June 1971. He got an apartment near my house and we continued working on our relationship. It was never the same after he moved, however. I tried so hard, but reality took over. I just couldn't make the final call with him. Deep in my heart I knew I had to let him go. He was homesick and that was obvious. He wanted to go home and see his friends and family. I don't blame him at all for his feelings. We were both young. I take the blame, if blame is to be had, because I felt it was me, all my fault. I broke our engagement on August 8, 1971. It was a very sad day for everyone. Brian was upset to say the least, but looking back I think perhaps he may have been a little relieved. He hadn't seen his family or friends or his hometown for quite some time. I wasn't ready to give him what he needed, and he in return was shadowed by something missing in his life. We were both lonely and in need of someone. We hung on to each other for the comfort and love that we both craved but it wasn't enough.

We weren't the only ones who felt the pain of our break-up. My dear brother Johnny had gotten really close to Brian. He was like a big brother to Johnny. I felt so bad for taking away his friend, his big brother, someone he loved. Johnny couldn't understand why I was making the choice I made. I really didn't expect him to, but needless to say he was hurt. He was angry with me for a while. I remember he cried when Brian left. I remember Johnny asking me, "Why do you have to break up with him?" I couldn't explain to an eleven-year-old what was really happening, though. I told Johnny I was so sorry, but that was little consolation for a boy who had not only lost his dad, but the best male friend he ever had. I told him that someday when he got older he would understand why I made the decision I did, and only then would he truly understand. He mourned Brian for quite a long time.

I knew I would never find another Brian. I hated myself, but I realized I felt relieved because I no longer felt trapped. I knew in my heart and in my head: marriage means divorce. I knew I needed help to change this way of thinking. Again I felt robbed of ever trusting anyone, and robbed of ever allowing myself to let go of the pain and deception I felt. I asked myself, *Who am I? I don't even know.*

Again I was alone. My sister was married, my younger sister had a steady boyfriend, and my mom (even after all those years of being alone) had a dear male friend. I felt empty and confused. I felt like my search for someone to love and to accept love from that person was beyond my reach. But I continued my journey. I never lost hope. Maybe, just maybe, I would be able to fall in love without any reservations.

I remember getting up the day after Brian left for home, and getting myself dressed and driving to work. I worked during the day, came home at night, and tried to act as if nothing had happened. I was frustrated that I couldn't get over the belief in my heart that relationships just don't work, and that a solid one was something I would never have. Why couldn't I just accept the fact that marriage just wasn't for me?

I will never forget Brian. He gave me love when I felt so unloved. He gave me promise. He liked me for me. He truly did. I often think about him, and I hope he is happy. He deserves it. I often think about what I would say if we were ever to cross paths again. I would tell him that he forever lives in my heart and he made my heart smile, and for this I will forever be grateful.

12

My Brother Johnny

My brother Johnny was born on September 10, 1959. He was beautiful, and he was *my* baby. I was ten years old. I remember that I loved taking care of him and that I pretended that he was mine. As he grew older we grew closer. We had a special bond. He was smart and wise beyond his young tender age. I enjoyed being his big sister. When I was older and got my license, I took him on drives with me. It was almost like we both had to escape with our thoughts. Sometimes we talked but often we just listened to the radio or the music on my eight tracks. It didn't matter what we did, the important thing was that we were together.

Johnny was only eighteen months old when our father left so he really never knew him. He also told me how wise he thought I was and he admired me, whatever he saw in me I sure couldn't see. Johnny was sensitive, kind, smart, and helpful, but he was also a very typical, mischievous boy. He loved riding his bike, and he and his friend often went on long rides unbeknownst to my mother. My mother always told him to stay close to home, only to find out that he rode his bike on several occasions to his friend's house, which was three miles away. He never did anything "bad" or mean, just innocent "boy stuff." He and my younger sister didn't get along too well. It might have been their ages or just regular sisterly-brotherly rivalries. My mom intervened often in their fighting, to no avail. On the other hand, Johnny was very protective of all of us. He was the "man of the house." He always protected my mom and make sure she was okay.

My mom had this occasional visitor; a male friend who we all saw had a liking for her. He didn't visit very often and my mom didn't feel the same about him. He had been a friend of my dad's and he did some carpentry work around our home. He was a master carpenter and did absolutely beautiful work. My mom was always kind to him and often offered him a cold drink on a hot day. It wasn't that he was nasty or inappropriate to my mom; she just wasn't interested in any kind of relationship with him, or anyone else for that matter. He owned a slaughterhouse in a neighboring town, which grossed us out. He would bring my mom meat that she never cooked for us. *Too gross,* we all thought. One afternoon he stopped by for a visit and unluckily for him my little brother was at home. Johnny knew my mom really didn't like this man but couldn't bring herself to tell him, so my brother took charge. I personally don't think Johnny liked the man, because he didn't wanted anyone taking his place as our mom's protector. After all, he was the man of the house. So, when he knocked on our door my brother was there to answer. He told this poor man to leave the premises of our home and never to come back. I remember his tone and it was clear from it that he meant what he said. As I said, my mom didn't really care for him, but still felt bad for him for whatever reasons she had. After my brother told him to take a hike, though, he never came back and we never saw him again.

Johnny helped my mom in a special way because he was a warm, sensitive young man whose compassion for people went beyond his own years. He had wisdom that usually comes with experience, and he had a way of making one feel special. He had a gift. He was unique and probably too good for this world. My mom had always wanted a boy, and with Johnny, after four girls, she finally got her wish. It was a dream come true for her, but her dream ended in a nightmare.

Johnny at Pleasure Island, Wakefield, MA

It was September 1972, and I was working at a local bank when Johnny's school nurse telephoned me after attempting, to no avail, to reach my mom. My brother was twelve years old then and had just entered eighth grade. She told me that Johnny had a very bad nosebleed and black and blue marks all over his body. This was quite frightening, and even more frightening because I had no idea what had caused his injuries. It turned out that a devastating disease was the culprit, one that left our family helpless and searching for answers. Johnny's sudden illness was one more thing our family didn't need, but quickly it far outweighed any other tragedy that we had already dealt with—it was an incomparable calamity.

I left work immediately to pick him up. When I got to the school the nurse told me that he should go right then to see a doctor. I asked her what was wrong with him, but she said very little, perhaps because my brother was standing next to me. I remember the drive home with Johnny. He told me how badly he felt. I tried to comfort him as much as I knew how but I knew something was drastically wrong. He looked so drained and he looked scared. I remember him telling me, "Jacqui, I feel so sick." He looked at me with great worry. I didn't know how I could help him. I didn't know what we were about to face. I felt helpless because I didn't know what was wrong. However, I did know that it wasn't good. I drove him home and waited impatiently for my mother to return.

As soon as my mom got home, I told her what had happened and we immediately brought my brother to his pediatrician. My mom's face showed much worry and concern but certainly she never expected what would soon transpire. The pediatrician told my mom that Johnny would have to go into the hospital for tests—immediately! We knew then that we were dealing with more than just a bad nosebleed. It was Friday evening the same day as his nosebleed when we took him to a local hospital where he had all kinds of tests, including x-rays, blood tests, et cetera. We spent a long night just waiting for the results of Johnny's tests. We didn't know what to expect. The next morning we got the results. *Johnny had leukemia.* Could this be true? We thought there had to be some kind of mistake. He had been so well only a couple of days before. He had just had a physical and had gotten the okay sign. He was fine. He had just started school.

Johnny had to be transferred to Massachusetts General Hospital in Boston from our local North Shore hospital. He was very weak by this time. My mom had to choose to have Johnny transferred by ambulance, or else she could take him to the hospital herself. This was no question: Johnny wanted my mom to take him, and he wanted me to be with him, too. I would not have had it any other way. The following morning we made the heartbreaking trip to Massachusetts General Hospital. The ride was long and painful for all of us. I was dying inside.

We arrived at Massachusetts General and parked the car. As we started our walk up to the overpass that lead to the hospital doors we saw that my husky brother didn't even have the strength to walk from the parking lot to the hospital entrance. The hospital building seemed so far away then. Johnny ran out of breath and could not continue his steps. I remember him saying to my mom, "I have to get in shape when I get out of here, Mom." He had to rest numerous times taking only about ten steps at a time. It broke our hearts. It felt so unreal.

A short time later, I remember my mom and I were brought into a conference room that, as much as I can remember, was very stark. Initially, Johnny was outside the conference room with the nurse while we met Dr. Truman. He wasted no time as he gave us the grave news. He told my mom and I that Johnny had acute leukemia, the *worst* possible kind. We were numb. This had to be a nightmare. But would we wake from it?

My mom mustered up the courage to ask the question that she feared might receive a devastating answer. "How long does Johnny have to live?"

The doctor replied, "Six weeks."

The anguish, hurt, and shock were unbearable. Johnny had not shown any symptoms of ill health. He had been given a clean bill of health at his physical four weeks prior to his bloody nose. It was indeed a nightmare, and we would never wake up from it. Meanwhile, Johnny had to be told.

When my brother came into the room after yet another test, he sat beside my mom and held her hand tightly. He knew he was about to be told very bad news. I could tell by the expression on his face how frightened he was. I felt helpless.

After the doctor told him the diagnosis, Johnny asked only, "Will I die?"

The doctor replied, "Yes, Johnny, you could die, but we will do everything possible not to let that happen."

Well, *I* died a thousand times. My mom died, too. *Why Johnny?* I asked. He was the best little boy in the world. We would not give up hope or our faith in believing that miracles happen. On September 10, three days after Johnny's nosebleed he celebrated his thirteenth birthday in a hospital bed.

The road to the end was long for Johnny. He received eight pints of blood on one day. He had to receive numerous transfusions from then on. Blood drives were held on his behalf to defray the outrageous costs. It didn't matter, though. What price on life is there? The leukemia entered his optic nerve on the third day of his hospitalization and blinded him. At first Johnny had tunnel vision but it progressed to just light shadows and then dark shadows. He suffered so much. He had to have brain surgery to take the pressure off his optic nerve, but it did not restore his sight. He never saw again.

Johnny never complained, not even once. He was a real trooper, and he intended to fight this terrible disease with his entire being. He would not give up, ever! The chemotherapy made him very sick and he lost all his hair within two weeks. His skin hurt and he struggled on to live. He wanted to get well. He wanted to be there for my mom. He was more concerned about who was going to take care of her than how very sick he was himself.

I remember one day in the fall when he was at a critical point. He called my mom over to his bedside. He then said, in a very peaceful tone, "Mom, I see Jesus. He's holding out his hands to me. He's saying, come, Johnny."

Johnny reached for the sky with open arms as if someone were indeed reaching for him. He had a smile on his face. I can still hear his words as if it were yesterday. I can't express well enough in words how I felt, how we all felt that day. He was so close to passing on and we all knew what his vision meant. We all thought that Johnny was going home to his Maker. But we didn't want him to leave us. We weren't ready for him to die. After staying by Johnny's side awhile, and after he had fallen asleep, our family visited the small chapel at the hospital and prayed to God for Johnny. We couldn't lose him. It wasn't fair. He was only thirteen years old and much too young to die, especially in such a horrible way. Through our prayers and strong faith in God we were granted a miracle, and God lent Johnny to us a little longer. Johnny made it through that critical time. We were so grateful. We were granted more time with Johnny. Looking back, I think that God was preparing us for what was to be, and I guess in a way ours was a selfish request but it didn't seem selfish at the time.

The road continued and was very rocky but Johnny improved. Johnny was still very ill from the course of chemotherapy, and was sick to his stomach the entire day after receiving it. We all felt so helpless in being unable to ease his pain. But, we all still wanted him to survive, and Johnny wanted to live, too. I believe he got his tenaciousness to live by knowing he had to get better to take care of my mom. He kept saying he was the man of the house and he was determined to keep it that way. He fought death with every ounce of his being and his spirit was strong.

Johnny was in remission. We thanked God for giving us more time. We wanted to believe that he was cured. Faith is what sustained us and hope is what we held in our hearts. He made it home for Thanksgiving, and what a Thanksgiving! He learned to walk again with a cane, he had a physical therapist, and I did physical therapy with him every day. He had a visiting nurse and an aide. His spirits were high. After Christmas, Johnny was back in regular school two days a week, and attended the Perkins School for the Blind three days a week. He had a Braille machine and learned basic Braille in no time at all. He was so smart and determined. He continued to receive chemotherapy and continued to be very ill from the side effects. On these days he was bedridden. Still, he never complained.

Johnny could never do enough for us in his eyes. He was more concerned and worried about us than himself. He wanted to make sure that we were okay. One

Saturday Johnny wanted to treat us to lobster pie from a local restaurant called Hilltop. It was known for its lobster and its quality and quantity. He insisted that he pay. My mom's dear friend Larry drove to Saugus to pick up the five lobster pies. I can still remember my brother's look of pleasure at being able to treat us to such an enjoyable dinner. This is how my brother was. He had a heart bigger than life itself. There sat my dear brother Johnny, not even being able to see, and yet making us happy was a little piece of heaven for him.

The joy we shared while Johnny was in remission was short lived. He had a relapse that following May and had to return to the hospital. This time he didn't get better. More chemotherapy, radiation, and countless tests were administered to him. It was more than anyone could bear, never mind a young boy. I think Johnny got tired. I think he got tired of the pain. I remember my mom telling us the night he died that they had given him morphine to ease the pain. My mom said that he called her to his side and asked, "Mommy, why didn't they give this to me before?"

Shortly after that, my brother took his last breath. My mom was there with him when he died. I can't even imagine how that must have been for her. I wished I could have been there for my mom and for Johnny. I always felt badly about not being there. I had spent that entire Sunday at the hospital with my brother and left that evening around 6:00 PM. My mom had wanted time to be alone with my brother so she had asked my sister and me to leave early that evening. My sister and I respected her wishes.

After my brother's death, his eighth grade class was getting ready to graduate. He had so much wanted to be part of it. I have always felt very badly that the school he attended could not grant him his only wish. My mom received a call after his funeral from Sister Superior. She asked my mom if she could meet with her in the chapel. My mom obliged. The Sister Superior handed my mom my brother's diploma. Why couldn't they have given it to *him*? Johnny died on May 28, 1973, never knowing that he indeed graduated with his class. He was buried on May 30, our mom's birthday.

One year to the day on May 28, 1974, at approximately 5:05 AM, our front door bell started to chime. I remember getting up to see who could be ringing our doorbell so early in the morning. When I arrived at the door no one was in sight. Our home was two hundred feet from the street. There was no way that anyone could have rung our doorbell and disappeared in such a short time span. And why would they want to? The only explanation I can understand is that my brother came back to let us know that he is okay, and for us to know that he is at peace and happy.

We all still miss him very much, but knowing that he is "alive" and well spoke volumes to us and gave us a sense of peace. Some may think it may have been a coincidence, and the doorbell had been malfunctioning, but how do they explain that the following year on May 28 at approximately the same time the same "coincidence" happened?

Our memories of Johnny will never die. He is with God, more alive than ever; watching over us and helping us stay strong. Little did I know that I would soon be drawing on his strength for an unexpected crisis of my own. I love you, Johnny.

This is part of a letter that we received from the Chaplain at Massachusetts General Hospital:

May 1973

To the family of Johnny:

I would like to express my sympathy at the passing on of John. Being he is so young and so good it's even more heartbreaking to lose him.

At the loss of a loved one we are deeply sad and often don't know how to begin again. I think of Mary under the cross of Christ on Calvary: her sorrow was very deep and yet she believed that He would somehow rise from the dead as He promised and as He promises for us. Faith and the realization those around her needed her more than ever helped her pick up the pieces and begin again.

We miss the presence of ones we love. Often we don't realize how much a loved one is part of our lives until we try to begin again without him.

John is still very much part of your family, pulling with and for you with God—he has gone ahead to help prepare your happy reunion in God's loving presence forever. At times like this God sometimes seems far away. We wonder why—why John? Why now? Why? I think that God cries too when He sees the entire human suffering. Yet through it all He pleads, "Trust Me, I love you. Things will work out. Love and not death will have the final word."

It is important to recall and share your memories of him. May God grant John the happiness of His loving presence forever and may God bless you abundantly too.

Sincerely,

Chaplain

Johnny 4 yrs old + friend Dean 6 yrs old

Johnny's First Communion 1964

David + Johnny

Johnny + neighbor David 1965

Debbie + Johnny 1966

13

Chris

In 1975 I met Chris. I was introduced to him through a friend of my sister. He was a fun-loving guy. I loved his smile. I was still amazed I could go out with someone who actually thought I was wonderful. From the start I felt that there was something special between Chris and me, and it just needed time to grow. I met Chris on the anniversary of my brother's death so I took this as a sign from my brother that Chris might be the one for me. I wanted this relationship to work, and this time I wanted to be sure about how I felt. However, I still had imbedded in my mind that no one could be trusted. I couldn't seem to trust anyone. I didn't know if it was my instinct telling me it wouldn't work, or my lack of ability to trust that was standing in the way. I wanted it to work and I willed that I would again try my best. Later on, I would find out that I always chose relationships that were safe. And even then, deep inside, I knew I would never be able to make the final step to marriage. After all, people who get married get divorced.

Chris loved me so much, and I knew he did. He was a pleaser. He wanted to make me happy and he enjoyed seeing me smile. I so much wanted to love him back. He was an electrician by trade and worked for a large electrical company on the North Shore. He lived in a neighboring city not far from me. He lived in his own apartment where he resided alone. He loved life and he loved boating. He owned his own speedboat, and during the summer of 1975 we spent many weekend days at his mom's home in Maine riding in it. His mom lived in a little cottage situated on a beautiful lake. The wide-open lake was picture perfect and wonderful for free-spirited rides. Chris took pride and joy in his speedboat and he loved sharing the good times with me. He enjoyed making me happy and would do anything for me.

I believed him when he told me how much he cared for me. His actions proved it. So, why I couldn't trust him? I wanted to so badly, but I could never get past the obstacles in my way. However, many things kept me holding on to that thread of hope because I wanted to believe he was the one for me. My brother Johnny had always been so concerned about me meeting someone nice. I also wanted to believe a loving relationship could happen to me again. I had already been engaged and it didn't work out. So now this had to be the right one, right? Like Brian before him, everyone loved Chris. He had a beautiful personality. He was always offering to help anyone who needed it. He was more than a really nice guy; Chris made me feel special. He would do anything for me. Why couldn't I feel for him like he felt for me? He made me feel needed, wanted, and loved, all of which felt good.

I tried to force the relationship. I didn't want to think anything negative, but I couldn't help it. I couldn't ignore the truth in my mind. The times I felt things were better were the times I blocked thoughts of abandonment and rejection out of my mind. . God, what was wrong with me? No one was perfect, so what was I looking for, and what was it I wanted instead? How could I not feel comfortable and sure with such a great guy? I didn't want to lose the love that I was getting from him, but after a while he wanted more from me. I knew I could probably never give him what he truly wanted: commitment! *Time will tell*, is what I kept telling myself.

We had great times together. His mom worked weekends as a nurse at the local navy base so we were able to enjoy her home alone, and did so occasionally with two other couples also. He got me to enjoy boating. I loved going with him for a cruise on the lake. On one of the Maine weekends we shared with our friends, the men decided to have a cookout for their ladies. They were going to do all the preparation and all of the cooking. We women just had to relax and enjoy. They made some delicious lemonade and gave us each a glass. It was cool and so refreshing. In fact, it was so good that we each had another glass, and then another. Little did we know that they had spiked the lemonade with vodka! It turned out to be a strange experience. I remember walking to the boat and tripping and wondering why I missed my step—*real funny*, I thought, as the guys roared with laughter. When we found out what those little connivers had done we were not too happy. But it was all in fun, and we did have a great day and weekend. During that summer we shared many good times. These times made memories that I will never forget.

One Christmas at his family's house, Chris surprised me with a gigantic box. It was wrapped in beautiful, colorful, festive wrapping paper. What could it be? I remember the fun we all had, especially me, as I opened the package only to find another wrapped package inside of the big box, and then another wrapped package in the smaller box, and so on. It was so much fun! Chris was laughing, his family was laughing, and I was, too. When I finally got through all the boxes and wrapping paper I was pleased to find a stereo unit. How beautiful. I loved it and was thankful for the really thoughtful and cherished gift. I loved the way he loved me. I loved his soft kisses and his warm embrace. He treated me with respect and I respected him.

Despite Chris's kindness, generosity, and love, I could not bring myself to make a total commitment to him. I'd always been honest with Chris from the beginning, letting him know that I didn't know if I could ever commit. I wanted to try, but at the same time it was important for me to be honest. I did not want to hurt him or lead him on.

The time came when I felt I needed to clear my head to make a decision whether to continue the relationship. I told Chris that I needed to take time away from him and think through things. Needless to say he was not too happy. Nevertheless, this was how it had to be. During our time apart Chris still wanted to talk to me. We didn't see each other, but we did talk. It wasn't what I wanted, and I didn't think talking was a good idea, but my fear of hurting him more than he was already feeling allowed me to have an occasional conversation with him. The breakup didn't last long, and I felt we never really had a break from each other, actually, because we still communicated with each other. After a month we decided to give it another try. I realized that I was trying to ignore the fact that Chris was very possessive and I felt trapped. I needed to feel in control of myself and I didn't feel that I was with Chris. This frightened me. I needed my space. I could not totally commit all my time to Chris, but I know this was what he wanted. He wanted me all to himself. I felt smothered and unable to breathe.

I had to make a final decision about us, in all fairness to him, and to me, for that matter. I felt pressured by him and it was really beginning to affect me. So I made the decision to end the relationship. It wasn't easy and Chris was relentless about hoping to change my mind. He sent me flowers and cards, he came to my work, and he called and visited me at my home. I was not pleased with his pursuit. If he had understood where I was coming from, I don't think he would have played his cards the way he thought would give him his "queen." He eventually gave up, but I know he never let go of me in his heart.

Absolutely, I have to say that Chris enriched my life in many ways. I really wish things could have been different. I prayed to God that someday He would send me someone I would be able to love, but also trust completely. This is something I knew that I had to work at, but I needed help doing it. I knew that my lack of trust in potential mates would inevitably always stand in my way of any relationship I ever would have. I just didn't know how to change. I often asked myself throughout my relationships, *Is it me? Am I the problem?* Why else had I sabotaged every romantic relationship that I experienced? I think I knew the answer, but I couldn't fix it. In my heart, I blamed my father, but I didn't want to feel resentment toward him so I pushed it out of my mind. How could I learn just to let it go instead? It was a lot deeper than that. It would turn out to take far more than "just letting go."

I realized that I could have made a grave mistake (twice) if I had gotten married for all the wrong reasons. I knew that many people got married for fear of being alone. These people got married even if it didn't feel right to them. They hoped in their hearts it would work anyway. It usually didn't, and ended in disaster, often involving helpless children. I could not and would not allow this to happen to me. I was in charge of my destiny, I thought, or at least wanted to be. I was determined to find out what it was, and who it was, I really wanted.

Values on life, sex, children, honesty, and so much more can break the foundation of love if the walls of a relationship aren't equally strong or at least the same structure. I loved Chris in a special way. We both would have ended up hurt. We had several different values. I wish him all the happiness in the world. He brightened mine, and I thank him for that. Chris will always remain in my heart, and I will always be grateful for how he enriched my life. I had wonderful times with him. He could make me smile, and even more than that, he could make me laugh, something that I didn't do very often. I hope he is happy, but one thing I am sure of: I am sure he is still boating.

14

College Life

It was July 1973 when I entered North Shore Community College with the intention of obtaining a degree in occupational therapy. I didn't have much hope of even being accepted into college, but I decided that I had nothing to lose by at least giving it a try. My passion was to help people less fortunate than myself. Occupational therapy sounded like an interesting field, and my work with children who had disabilities had made this kind of profession very appealing to me. The college was fairly new then, as it had first opened in 1965. It was small, and everyone knew each other. My first impression was how friendly everyone seemed. Even the building had character, to say the least.

The first person I met was the Dean of Continuing Education. He was so pleasant and so amicable. I have always believed the first person you meet when walking for the first time into a store, business, school, or any new environment is the impression that you get for the entire place. He gave a great first impression. He was very personable and he showed a great interest in *me*. He told me about the college and all about the great academic programs that the college offered. I told him my interests and expressed my concerns about even entering college to him. He tried to ease my fears. It worked: I was excited and felt a thread of hope. I told him I was interested in the occupational therapy program and that I had worked with an occupational therapist at my job. I had liked what she did and the results that she had accomplished. He checked the status of the program, and to my dismay the program was already filled for the fall semester. He told me that the program was very popular and that they only accepted eighteen students a year. He told me not to get discouraged, and that he had a plan for me. Little did I know that this would prove to be the beginning of a new and long-lasting adventure.

The dean spoke to me about a position that was open at the college in the financial aid office. He told me they were in need of a secretary, and it was a full-time position. One of the benefits was that I could attend college free of charge.

He told me I could start right away by taking the core classes needed for any degree. I could take these classes in the evening or perhaps during lunch. He also assured me that there were counselors who could assist me in the process. Wow! I couldn't believe how he was going out of his way for me ... *me! This would be perfect for me*, I thought. He gave me the name of the director of financial aid to set up an appointment. I had no idea what this entailed, but I made the phone call. I was nervous and I remember dialing the number hoping that I would sound intelligent enough for him to want to meet with me.

When I spoke to the director of financial aid he said he wanted to meet with me to discuss the possibility of hiring me to work with him. He set up an interview. I remember feeling a bit nervous, but nonetheless I was excited that this just might be a brand-new start for me. I hoped that he liked me when we met face-to-face. I had nothing to lose. In fact, he liked me from the start. The interview turned out to be very casual and I felt quite at ease with the entire process. I got the job. It sounded like an exciting position and was full of promise, even more so because I could also begin my journey as a college student, taking one course at a time if I wished. I couldn't believe it: I had a job that instinctively I knew I was going to like and soon I would start school. Mr. H, the Director of Financial Aid, wanted me to start immediately, and time was of the essence. He had not had a secretary for a while, and was anxious to get someone on board. He seemed very nice, well mannered, and professional. I think what impressed me the most about him was that he had confidence in me that I couldn't even see for myself. He let me spread my battered wings.

I started working in the financial aid office in July of 1973. The work was exciting and interesting; and, for once, I felt that I could make something out of my life. I wanted to make my mother proud of me. The funny part about this new position was that I didn't know anything regarding financial aid or anything about college life for that matter. The director, however, believed in me. He arranged for me to attend financial aid workshops and seminars. He allowed me to attend a conference that was held at a university in Boston at which I met other people who were directly connected with financial aid. He personally took an interest in making sure that I was okay. This period in my life was probably was the first time I looked at myself and reasoned, *Maybe you are not as stupid as you feel.* Here stood a professional who had faith in me and believed in me. It felt great!

One of my first experiences at the college ended up being quite humorous. An instructor shared space with me within the financial aid office. It was my first summer of working at the college so I wasn't familiar with the terminology. I was told that if anyone came in looking for Mr. S. to tell him or her that Mr. S. was on leave for a *sabbatical.* I, being unfamiliar with college terminology, heard *safari.* Needless to say during the entire summer when people asked me where Mr. S. was, I proudly told them he went on a safari. It wasn't until the fall of the 1973 semester that I learned the truth, when I asked Mr. S. how interesting it must have been to explore the depths of Africa and the wild life. The look on his face spoke volumes. I knew something was radically wrong. Embarrassed? That was an understatement. He politely told me that he had been on a sabbatical and not a safari. Every time he came into the office all I could think about was what I had been telling people, and what they must have thought of me, when they, too, learned the truth. I knew I could not let an experience like this happen again, but it did!

I had so much to learn about working at a college and working in the financial aid office. Financial aid can be very confusing and it is very detailed. It has many rules and regulations that have strict guidelines that must be adhered to. It is very important to know what the guidelines are in order to follow through correctly. I learned the hard way what a Student Financial Aid Statement (S.F.S.) was versus a Parents Confidential Statement (P.C.S.). A student with a very strong southern accent came into the Financial Aid office and asked me for a "PCS" Parent's Confidential Statement. At the time, I had been working in the office less than a week. I did not even know what a Parents Confidential Statement was. Meanwhile, I had heard this man say, "Can I have a piece of your A__(PCS)?" Well, the look on my face frightened him, to say nothing of what I was feeling! I couldn't believe my ears. I couldn't believe what he had just said to me. After what seemed to have been forever, he glanced over at the shelf, walked over and picked up a form, which turned out to be a Parents Confidential Statement, not a "piece ah ass" at all. He gave me a look I will never forget and left the office.

I decided I needed to learn the lingo of the college life. I began to do some homework to learn about financial aid as quickly as I could. During that summer, the director of financial aid helped me apply to become a notary public, since at the time students had to have their signatures notarized before receiving their financial aid award checks. I learned a ton and I was really getting to like the position. I was accepted as a notary public for the state of Massachusetts and received my first commission for seven years.

The financial aid office was approved for a work-study student. This was when I met my good friend Terri. She added so much humor to the office. She was quick-witted and very smart. She helped me type letters to be sent to students and signed them putting "Assistant to the Assistant" under her name. This was pretty funny; since neither of us had big titles we invented our own. She greeted the students and helped me with the constant traffic that came into the office. Terri is still a great friend of mine today, and she still has her great sense of humor.

The following September I registered for an anatomy and physiology class at the college. I still hoped to enter the Occupational Therapy program. I loved working with people, I knew, but a doubt about whether I wanted to still pursue occupational therapy had begun to grow. I loved my job working in the Financial Aid office. The director was pleased with me, but mostly I was happy because I was doing what I wanted to do, which was to help people. It was in a totally different vein than I had expected that I found this fulfilling work, but this was starting not to matter to me. The point was to help individuals and this is what I was doing. My job gave me a sense of some self worth, and gave my life purpose.

The anatomy class consisted of nursing students and me. Nursing students needed to take the course for their program, and I needed it for occupational therapy, assuming I might still head that way. I admit, I could not grasp the course work. I had not even taken biology in high school so I had no knowledge of even the basics and this course was advanced. I couldn't even pronounce some of the words, never mind understand what they meant. I was in big trouble! I had no experience in the world of science. I decided that since I could not handle anatomy and physiology, I would probably never be accepted into any such rigorous program that required it. At this point I had decided that occupational therapy wasn't what I wanted anymore. I was happy where I was. I should concentrate on what I was doing at the time. I am glad I realized this early on into my path of study. Should I attempt college in another vein? I didn't want to give up my aspirations for college completely, but I didn't want to give up my job working in the financial aid office, either.

I loved kids and had enjoyed working with them. I knew there was a connection between us. Maybe exploring that interest would lead me to a good avenue for my talents. I looked into the Early Childhood program. It sounded really interesting, and its courses were also offered in the evening division of the college. It also didn't have any science requirements. I was thankful for that! I applied, and was accepted into the program. I was thrilled. I continued working full time and attended college at night. I received 'experience' credit for my previous work and, course-by-course, I worked my way through the curriculum. I worked at a local preschool for one semester, putting in ten hours per week to complete my internship. It took me longer than it would have if I had gone full time, but that was not an option for me. Anyway, I enjoyed the journey.

I graduated in 1979 with honors. Wow, I couldn't believe it! I had never thought I would be able to attend college. I had never been encouraged, nor could I afford to attend. I didn't think I was capable of succeeding. I had only had negative feelings, but that changed when I found myself working at the college. I was able to concentrate on my coursework and enjoy the journey rather than look ahead to a job out there for me after graduation.

Since I had graduated from the program in Early Childhood, I thought I should at least explore the possibilities of getting a job in that field of study. However, pay at that time was six dollars an hour, tops. I couldn't afford to take a pay cut. If I went on for my full bachelors degree and obtained a job in the field, I wouldn't make much more, and I couldn't afford to do that, anyway. I loved my job at North Shore Community College, and I realized more than ever that I was helping lots of kids. It wasn't what I thought I'd be doing, but still I was doing what I loved. After researching salaries in the field of Early Childhood I decided that the pay at the time was not substantial enough for me.

The director of financial aid left the college in 1975. I was very concerned about who would take his place. Could I be so lucky as to have it be someone who believed in me as he had? Fortunately for me, a guardian angel was watching over me. I found myself working for a new director and assistant director. They became like family. I loved both of these guys. Bob, the new director, was so nice and so supportive. He continued to afford me the opportunity to learn and progress. Jim, the assistant director, became the dad I really never had. We became very close and I became very attached to him and his family. Bob and Jim allowed me to join them while attending conferences, social events, and so forth. They invited me to join them at a meeting they attended at a local high school. I met the school's director of counseling there and learned much about the Northeast Counselors Association organization to which both Bob and Jim belonged. The director of guidance who was also the president of the Northeast Counselors Association was very impressed with me and asked me if I would like to join his organization. Its mission was helping students find the colleges that best suited their needs. I am still a member today, serving on the Board as the Vice President of Post Secondary Colleges. My job could not have been better. I loved it and loved my colleagues. I was also spreading my wings.

However, "my family" fell apart in 1984. Bob left the college then and my "dad" Jim had a massive heart attack. Unfortunately, Jim didn't make it. I was devastated. I had loved him. He had been so good to me. Again, someone I had attached myself to was no longer in my life. I was broken hearted. Before he died, I visited Jim at the hospital where he lay in a coma. I remember talking to him and although he could not speak I know he knew I was there. We all lost a great person the day he left the earth. I believe he is looking down on all the people he loved and all the people who loved him sending us his love and comfort.

The new director had a different vision on how the financial aid office should be run. All my responsibilities changed and I was no longer doing what I so loved. Bob and Jim had given me such opportunities. My confidence with this new director dwindled. I had worked so hard to get where I was and now I felt I was tumbling to the bottom. In addition to being devastated by losing "my family" in financial aid, I felt lost wondering what would happen to me next. I needed to try something new so I asked for a transfer. It turned out to be a blessing because it opened up another door for me and I got to experience another dimension of college life.

I transferred to another office but my heart was broken and I felt empty. I had lost most of my confidence. Many old scars that I thought were fading felt torn open again. I needed a break. I needed time to heal from the loss of my "buddies" Jim and Bob and the loss of a job I had so loved. With the wonderful help and guidance from the dean of the college I decided to take a leave of absence from my job for the summer and return in the fall. It was the best decision that I could have made. I thoroughly enjoyed my summer traveling, going to the beach, relaxing, and getting healthy again. I realized that I had so much bottled up stress that needed to be released and it had such a strong hold on me, that without this break I probably would have ended up very ill. I had gotten so much support from North Shore Community College and the dean who made it happen. They stood by me all the way. I felt so fortunate, and was amazed at the same time that they cared. They truly cared about me.

When I returned at the beginning of the fall semester my new "home" was in the Placement office. I loved the job and worked with a fantastic man there named Dominic who was the director of the placement office at the college. He welcomed me warmly. I knew I would be happy there. I couldn't wait to begin. I was ready. He was warm and caring, and we worked well as a team. Once again I felt my confidence slowly return. He allowed me to make decisions, and he allowed me to grow. He provided me with opportunities that I whole-heartedly accepted. Working in the placement office was so different than the financial aid office, and I liked the changes and the challenge. I enjoyed helping students find jobs and I enjoyed working with employers to find the right person for the job opportunity they were presenting. It was fun. Also, I met a woman who became a very good friend of mine. Sandy didn't work for the Placement office but had a desk there where she did her job.

Dominic and I became very good friends and I would often visit him and his wife Agnes at their home. They were terrific people. They were special people. I remember Dominic talking about adopting a child. He had done a lot of research on adoption and he and his wife had enormous love to give to a special child. It seemed like forever, but the day finally came when their dream came true. It came true not only once, not twice, but three times and all at once! They adopted three brothers from Costa Rica. How special is that! The boys were very young. They were all under six years of age. They spoke only Spanish but communication was not a problem. The love that Dominic and Agnes had for those boys broke the language barrier.

My friends and I at the college gave them a "kids" shower. Dominic had taken time off to help the boys adjust to their new life. I had asked Dominic to pick a time when we could all meet his new family. Little did he and his wife know what was awaiting them: they thought they were coming to the college to bring the boys to meet everyone, and they were but ... *Surprise!* They were indeed happily surprised when they walked into the room and saw everyone anxiously awaiting their arrival. They received great gifts, and we presented them with a check for $1,500 dollars! It was a joyous occasion to say the least.

The Placement office took on an entirely new role, which led me to the best experience of my college career: working in the Counseling Center. I loved working with students, and this new position gave me even more of an opportunity to do what I loved doing. It was there that I was encouraged to obtain my bachelor's degree in counseling by a co-worker named Anita. She also encouraged me to go on from there for my master's degree. *What was she thinking? I could never do that! Or could I?* The number of people who believed in me at North Shore Community College still amazes me today. At that point I continued working, but was still interested in taking classes, remembering Anita's encouraging words. After taking a few psychology classes I found that I continued to be interested in this field. I knew I didn't want to leave North Shore Community College but I knew I wanted to continue my education and receive my bachelors degree.

It was 1984, and I was ready to complete my educational mission. I researched the different programs available to someone who wanted to work full time and attend classes in the evening. I knew I wanted to receive my degree in counseling, but needed to determine what type of counseling to pursue. I found a program that met my needs, and enrolled at University of Massachusetts-Amherst (UMASS Amherst) in a program called University Without Walls. This was a program for which you could attend evening classes, and, with the help of an advisor, design your own degree. A friend and colleague of mine named Lil also wanted to continue her education. Lil and I applied to the college at the same time and we both were accepted. We met with an academic advisor in the University Without Walls program. His name was Rick, and he was so nice. We each explained what our interests were and he helped us tailor the program to our choosing.

I chose financial aid/career counseling as my major. I thought since I already knew so much about financial aid that this would be a great way to advance in the field. I felt it would open yet another door for me if I was ever to pursue a career in financial aid. I could use my skill and knowledge at the college. My friend chose gerontology as her major. It wasn't an easy task for either of us, but we were both motivated at the time. We set our sights on accomplishing our goals and we were both tenacious enough not to let anything stand in our way. I didn't want to disappoint anyone and I didn't want to embarrass myself. I would not give up, nor would she. Classes were held at the UMASS Medial Building, a satellite school of the University of Massachusetts Amherst in Worcester, west of Boston. Each week after completing our full-time jobs, we traveled to Worcester for classes. We traveled from Beverly to Worcester religiously once and sometimes twice a week. The travel time took about one hour and fifteen minutes, or longer in inclement weather. We left our jobs at 4:00 PM and usually arrived by 5:30 PM. This left less than a half hour to grab a bite to eat, because classes were usually held from 6:00 PM until 10:00 PM. It was indeed a long day, only to have to report to work the very next morning. It didn't matter. Through rain, sleet, snow, and occasionally nice weather we drove to Worcester to complete our degrees course by course. It took a good three years, but we did it. I graduated in 1987 with high honors.

Now it was time for my master's degree. Could this be possible? I applied to Salem State College not really knowing what to expect. I was accepted to a master's program, much to my amazement, and started my journey to earn my degree in psychological services/counseling in 1993. It was long, but worth it. I owe a great deal of thanks to Dr. Underwood, who helped me through the process of obtaining my master's degree. Dr. Underwood has to be one of the nicest people I have ever known. He had worked in the Counseling Center at North Shore Community College with me, and he was always there to lend me a helping hand. With Dr. Underwood's help and guidance I completed all of my courses in the evening division after working hours. Unfortunately he passed away from a massive heart attack just before graduation; he is sorely missed. In the end, I enjoyed my journey, and going on to get my degrees was one of the best decisions I have made in my life. I met many people and grew a lot while learning from them. I graduated from the Psychological Services/Counseling program with high honors in May 1997.

The next step was to work toward getting my (LMHC) License Mental Health Counselor status. I had to complete 2000 hours of work and pass the State Board of Massachusetts examination to earn it. I remember studying for the exam with my friend Jenn. I worked two evenings a week in the Counseling Center during that time, too. This was quite enjoyable; however, tiring because I had already worked a full day. It was worth it in the end. A great friend and supervisor named Judy helped in the process of guiding me through my 2000 hours.

Jenn and I tested each other relentlessly. The exam was given in Boston and was four hours long. I remember how very stressed I was taking the exam. Then waiting for the results seemed to take an eternity. The day I ripped open the envelope and saw a big "P" (for "pass") was one of the best days of my life.

After receiving my license in psychological services counseling through the State of Massachusetts, I worked my way into a professional position. I work currently as an academic counselor at the college and serve students with their academic needs, which include college adjustments and very often issues of personal concern. I am doing what I love.

College was new to me when I began my journey, and it opened up a brand-new world. I owe a lot to North Shore Community College. It gave me wings, wings that had been broken. I believe my brother Johnny led me there. He was always concerned with my happiness, and wise beyond his years. I still feel Johnny's presence. I asked him to guide me and help me. He did. He was my angel, and to this day guides me along the rocky paths of life. He is my shining star.

15

Surviving Cancer

In 1976, while participating in an exercise class at a local health club, I noticed a huge eight inches in length and four inches deep lump on the calf of my left leg. I didn't pay much attention to it and passed it off as a muscle sprain from vigorous exercise. It started to concern me after a month because it wasn't going away, and in fact it was getting larger. I consulted the health club instructor. She told me that she also thought it was probably a muscle sprain and I could work it out with physical massage. I tried, but to no avail. I continued to exercise vigorously every-day but it was still getting larger. I knew at this point that it was more than a muscle sprain. Muscle sprains, to my knowledge, don't grow. I made an appoint-ment with my doctor to find out what I could do. It had been over a month since I had first noticed the lump.

My dear mom came with me. As my doctor examined my leg, I knew that it wasn't going to end with his simple observation. Sure enough, Dr. McGilvrary wanted me to go to my local hospital for tests. This frightened me. The next morning, May 1, my mom took me to the hospital. I waited anxiously for my test results, and then instead of getting them I was admitted to the hospital. I couldn't believe that I had to be hospitalized. I was scheduled for all kinds of additional tests, from blood tests to X-rays, EKG, EEG, and numerous other screenings. Some of the tests were quite painful. I felt like a pincushion. I didn't know what to expect, and I was fearful of what was to come, but no answer came.

I was shown to my room and told to undress and get into bed. I was not allowed to get up or move around. This was very disturbing. I still didn't know what was going on. It turned out that they thought I might have a blood clot, and so it would be very dangerous for me to move. How could I have a blood clot? I remember praying and asking God to help me through this ordeal. I couldn't believe this was happening. It was so surreal. I wanted to wake up from this nightmare, but instead this was the beginning of a long, painful journey that would change my life forever.

The doctors decided to biopsy my left leg. Even with the results of a complete set of tests they couldn't find anything conclusive. I went into surgery not knowing what to expect or what they would find. I had no idea what I was about to be told. After three weeks in the hospital, I received the word: *cancer*. The pathology report described "a poorly differentiated spindle cell sarcoma with multiple mitotic figures." Amputation was considered the best option for saving my life. They searched to see if metastases were present; if so, there would be no point of amputating because my life span would be too short. The likelihood of metastases was great because of the rate of growth of the tumor. Fortunately no metastases were found and they decided to administer multimodality therapies, including surgery, chemotherapy, and irradiation, which could spare a person from losing a limb. Some of this information was included in my case history, which appeared in the September 1977 edition of the *Hospital Practice Journal*, written by my oncologist Dr. J. Lokich.

The morning after this battery of tests had been administered, I received a visit from Dr. McGilvrary. He told me I had a very rare type of cancer. There had been only seven other documented cases of this type of cancer. He told me that he had done extensive research to find out how he could help me. Miraculously, he found Dr. Suit, who was a doctor at a Massachusetts General Hospital and had found treatment for this rare form of cancer. Because my cancer was so aggressive, treatment had to begin immediately. I had little or no chance of survival if this treatment didn't work. If I was not improving and the drugs had little or no effect they would not amputate. I could live the short time I had left with my leg. I slowly digested this news. I can't explain the entire thought process I went through, perhaps because I was numb to the whole experience.

I remember it as if it were yesterday, though. My mom came into the hospital room. She told me I had a good chance of surviving and that they were going to do all they could to make sure that happened. I could tell that my prognosis wasn't good. I could see in her face that she wasn't being totally honest with me. She wanted to spare me, but of what I wasn't sure. One thing I was certain about was that I had already heard the worst news from the doctor? I remembered lying in bed that night in disbelief. *How did I get cancer? How could this be?* I remember thinking that it was my fault. All the years of bottled up frustration had taken a toll on my body. All the pain and all the hurt that I held inside and could never let go of had finally collected into this tumor. I had never allowed myself to get angry. I felt guilty about everything I did, and now I had to pay the price. I had to purge the bad out of my body. It had to come out some way. I actually felt that maybe I would be a better person from this experience *if* I survived. I wanted to be a better person. I would offer up my suffering to God. If I didn't survive from the treatment I was about to receive to cure the cancer then maybe I would have paid the price to earn my way to heaven.

I thought about my brother Johnny. I thought about how much he had suffered. He never did anything wrong; he was a good boy and a wonderful brother. How could two people in the same family experience such a devastating illness? I prayed. When I was told that I had cancer and could die I asked Johnny to be by my side and help me through the ordeal ahead of me. I prayed to the Sacred Heart of Jesus, the Blessed Mother of God, and St. Jude. I made a promise to the Blessed Mother that if I survived I would make a pilgrimage to Lourdes (a shrine in France) in thanksgiving to her. It is amazing, though; I didn't cry. I was going to be strong. This cancer was in for a big fight. It wasn't so much about surviving, as I said I wasn't sure if I even wanted to live, but more out of principle about not letting evil win. Evil had taken over too many times ... no more. I must admit that I actually welcomed death for moments during this period. It found a peaceful place within me. It offered a chance that my pain might disappear with my life. I wasn't afraid to die. *How nice it must be on the other side. It had to be better than this side.* It was an unfair world that seemed to win a lot with no consequences.

When my friends found out that I had been afflicted with cancer it was interesting to see how they responded to such horrible news. A few of my friends avoided me. I wanted to understand their distance and tried to put myself in their shoes. I realized they probably felt uncomfortable and didn't know what to say. The fact is they didn't have to say anything at all. Just knowing that they were there for me would have meant everything. I don't think they wanted to see me sick, pale (totally noticeable for me), and with no hair. They couldn't cope. They probably thought it could be them lying in that hospital bed. I certainly don't hold that against them. I can only imagine how difficult it must have been for them. I am sure it bothered them to stay away, too.

However, many of my friends sent their warm thoughts through cards and gifts. I truly appreciated that. It brought a smile to my face and a feeling of support and care. Some close friends visited me in the hospital and supported me in any way that they could. This meant the world to me. My dear work friends traveled together into Boston to visit me. I appreciated all their effort and know that it was not an easy task. Boston was over twenty miles away, but after a long day at work they still found the time to visit me. Once with me, they shared some of their experiences getting into Boston through crazy traffic patterns, which gave me a chuckle. They were such great friends and are to this very day.

One of the test administered to me put me through the most excruciating physical pain I had ever experienced. It felt like my leg was being sawed off, slowly. The cancer, though, this test showed, had not spread to my bones, which was a very positive thing. I met with the oncologist who proceeded to tell me about the method of treatment that they were going to administer to me. The ill effects it would have on my body were devastating but this course of drugs could possibly save my life. Did I have a choice? I remember when Dr. Lokich told me that I would lose all of my hair due to the chemotherapy treatments. I was scared and devastated. I was also told that the drugs could make me sterile and that I would be physically sick. Moreover, they could affect other vital organs but they would keep close tabs on me by administering yet more tests. *So, now tell me something positive,* I thought.

I started my chemotherapy treatments on May 17, 1976 at the Dana Farber Cancer Institute. I will never forget that day. I didn't know what was in store for me and it probably was a good thing. The nurses at this hospital were fabulous. One nurse, whose name was Cathy, was particularly compassionate. She held my hand and explained everything that was about to happen. She never left me in the dark. I was terribly sick afterward, and I could actually feel myself getting sick during the treatments. I was so afraid. The doctor certainly was right about the side effects, but there was no way I could have envisioned that it would be as bad as it was. My mom drove me to the hospital for my first treatment of chemotherapy that included Cyclophosphamide with Doxorubicin (Adriamycin) and the less familiar Dacarbazine (Dimethyltriazenyl Imidazole Carboxamide, or DTIC). This combination of drugs had a 50% response rate. It was worth a try, fifty-fifty. All of the nurses were very nice and comforting, and took the time to explain to me what they were doing. As they put the intravenous needle into my arm a great fear came over me. First of all, it took them a while to find a good vein. My veins were small so it made it tapping them difficult. I felt helpless. I could have said "forget it, I don't want this," but then evil would have won (but I wondered if it was winning anyway). I remember I kept telling myself that evil might be winning the battle but it wasn't going to win the war. I prayed the entire time that I sat in that chair as the "poison" trickled through my veins. I held tight onto my faith that God is all good and He is helping me through this every step of the way. I thought of my brother Johnny and thought of the pain and agony he endured with such bravery. I asked him to help me, too, and I knew he would. If anyone had a direct line it would be him.

I used to have these horrible nightmares of someone kidnapping me and turning me into a heroin addict and then releasing me without my drug. In these nightmares, I was forced into prostitution because I had to support my habit. I needed the drug and the power of the drug stole my soul. In my nightmare I was terrified of the heroin because it took over my life and controlled me. I had no way out. It had me captured. It was as if I was in the middle of a field with burning flames surrounding me. I felt the same way as I awaited my first chemotherapy treatment and every chemotherapy treatment after that.

It always took them a while to find a good vein to insert the painful needle into my arm. As the drug entered my veins, I began to feel the nausea coming on. It got worse, and never got better. I was sick for eleven hours straight with vomiting and dry heaves. I felt dead. My skin actually hurt. It is difficult to describe how skin hurts but it was as if all my nerve endings were exposed and someone was blowing on my skin. The worst part was that my treatments were scheduled for two days in a row every three weeks. This meant that after the vomiting finally stopped, I had to return the very next day for a new set of drugs, which affected me in the same way. This time I was *only* sick for nine hours. I remember being told that these treatments could affect my nerves, liver, and heart. But, this was the only option I had. If I took the drugs then I might live, and if I didn't take them I would die. I received treatments for twelve months.

During the course of my chemotherapy treatments I also received radiation. I went into the hospital Monday through Friday for six weeks to receive my dose of radiation. Part of my radiation treatment required hospitalization, which included "catheters that were used to implant yttrium beads in the tumor bed that would raise the total local radiation dose to 7,500 rads." (*Hospital Practice*, September 1977) This was surgically done. In layman terms, live radiation was implanted in my leg and would gradually release its dose of radiation to kill the cancer. During my radiation treatments when the rads were inserted into my leg, I had to be isolated from other patients, staff, and visitors. It really did feel strange to feel that it was dangerous for others to get near "radioactive" me.

I was eventually able to go back to work. I worked fewer hours during the weeks I received my chemotherapy treatments. I was extremely tired but I was lucky enough to work at a college and have a boss who understood my precarious situation. Because of my surgery I had to use a cane to assist me in walking. I remember walking up this slight hill that seemed like a mountain to me. I felt like everyone was looking out their office windows as I slowly approached the door to the college and carefully ascended the stairway to my office. There were no elevators in the over one-hundred-year-old building in which the college resided. I had no choice but to climb the stairs to my destination. I was determined to do this and not make a big deal out of it. I did make it up the stairs and was happy that I could. I was thankful that I could go back to work.

It was totally devastating to lose all my hair. I wanted to believe that this was one side effect that would not afflict me. I prayed for this not to happen. My hair was quite long then, and I remember one evening taking a bath and washing my hair. As I rubbed my fingers through my hair, giant chunks of it fell into my hand. I lost all of my hair within two weeks. I was bald. My anxiety over lost hair had nothing to do with vanity. I felt like I was losing part of myself, like a person afflicted with leprosy may feel losing part of his or her body. I couldn't believe that I had not one hair on my head. I lost the hair over my entire body. If I had to look for one positive thing through this entire experience maybe it was that I didn't have to shave my legs, underarms, or take care of any facial hair.

My mom and I shopped for a wig. The lady who helped us was so nice. I remember her because she was so compassionate. My mom bought me a very nice wig that gave me longer hair than I ever had. It did look real but I knew it wasn't. I felt like everyone knew I had a wig, especially people who knew what I was going through. The people at work were very nice to me. They were warm and caring and I felt their compassion, but I just wanted this ordeal to be over. At least my hair would grow back after the chemotherapy treatments ceased. I couldn't wait until the day that my treatments were over. I worried that they may have to extend them, and I worried that they may not even prove to be effective. I was one big worry-wart, afraid how all of this would affect me. I could not bear to think of going through the horrendous treatments of chemotherapy again. I tried to put that thought out of my mind, but it wasn't easy.

I was truly blessed in that the treatment did miraculously work for me. The tumor had encapsulated. I finished my last chemotherapy treatments on April 6, 1977. The next step was to remove the tumor that the drugs had shrunk to a much smaller size. They scheduled my surgery to remove it. The doctors said they got all of the cancer, but only time would tell if I would suffer a relapse. I remember asking the doctors if I was cured from cancer. I remember asking if I could ever get another type of cancer, too, and unfortunately they said I could. I didn't want that to stand in the way of this most joyous time of recovery, but I needed to know if it could come back. It has now been over thirty years that I have been cancer free.

I'm thankful for the wonderful doctors and nurses, and for my faith in God that helped me through those tough times. If I didn't believe that there was life after death and that there truly is a God, I know in my heart I wouldn't have fought so hard. My mom supported me all the way. She loved and cared for me. I had a lot of other help, too. A gentleman named Dick from the Red Cross drove me quite often to Dana Farber hospital for my treatments. A wonderful neighbor, Mrs. D., stayed with me when my mom had to be at work. My Aunt Gert helped when she could, and many people cared in so many other ways.

I fought against this cancer for my brother, Johnny, who I felt was right beside me the entire time. I gained my strength from him. If a thirteen-year-old boy could bear the devastating effects of this terrible disease, lose his sight, lose his hair, be deathly ill, and survive brain surgery and endless bone marrow tests, then so could I.

I offered up my suffering to God and knew it was not in vain. I was able to see something positive in this grueling nightmare. I was actually thankful that I didn't have kidney disease that would keep me on dialysis or a chronic illness that I would have to live with for my entire life. No, I was quite lucky. If I could survive this then I could go on with my life. I held on to the thread of hope that maybe I had won a new beginning. If I died, it wouldn't matter anyway. I would be going to a better place where angels fly and my brother and grandmother would be there to greet me at the door.

16

Moving Out

I was twenty-nine years old, and I still lived at home. I wanted to be on my own so badly, but I was guilt-ridden that I would be leaving my mom alone. I felt like I would be deserting her after all she had done for me. I would be the last one to move out. My two sisters were married so that had been their excuse for leaving, but what was mine? I had freedom, my mom didn't have me on curfew anymore, we got along great, and I had my own room. So what was my problem?

I struggled with this for quite sometime but I finally came to terms with it. The fact was that if I didn't move out, I wouldn't feel the independence that I so badly needed. I might even become resentful of my mom, and I certainly didn't want that to happen. I was torn. Leaving my mom meant she would no longer have the income that I gave toward rent to live in her home because I would have to put that money toward rent for my own place. On the other hand, I felt trapped and frustrated. I made the decision to move on. I started my search for a place of my own.

I didn't know what to expect. I called several real estate agents to assist me with my search. The real estate agencies were not that interested in helping me find an apartment. They were more concerned with people who wanted to buy or sell houses. I was used to doing things on my own anyway, so I ventured out myself. It was exciting for me to have finally made such a tough decision, and I was glad to be acting upon it. I was more than ready.

I bought several local newspapers and searched the "apartments for rent" section. In the local *Salem Evening News* I found an advertisement for a small apartment in Salem, MA. It gave the street location so I knew where it was located. It was in a nice area of the city. I was very familiar with Salem and its surroundings. I liked the area a lot and could easily visualize moving there. I telephoned the number in the ad and a woman answered the phone. I told her that I was interested in looking at the apartment she had listed for rent. She told me it was on the second floor of her residence. We talked for a while and she seemed interested to meet me. She seemed to be very nice and had a pleasant voice. Since I was working in the neighboring town, I was only about fifteen minutes away from where the apartment was located. I made an appointment to meet her and see the apartment during my lunch hour.

I arrived at her house and knocked at her door. She opened the door and I introduced myself. I will never forget the look on her face. I felt as if she stripped me with her eyes. I didn't know if I had grown another head, or if I had forgotten to dress, or what. A look of horror appeared over her face. The next thing that came out of her mouth was astonishing. She asked me, "Are you *I*talian or something?"

I couldn't believe my ears and my heart sank. She pronounced the "I" as if it were some horrible thing.

I replied, "Yes, I am of Italian and French decent."

She said nothing but continued to stare me down.

I knew in my heart that she had no intention of renting me the apartment. The expression on her face and the tone of her question had said it all, but apparently she had more to say.

"I don't rent to *I*talians!" again making a distinct *I* sound. "They are filthy, dirty people and I don't rent to *I*talians!" she repeated, as if she needed to tell me again.

Her cruel tone and hateful words brought back memories of so very long ago from the nun that morning in the Catholic school bathroom. Alright already, she doesn't rent to Italians, I got the picture. I was beyond hurt; I was devastated by her comments. Here I was, an adult still feeling the pain of prejudices I had felt as a child. Would I ever escape the prejudices? Once again I wanted to be invisible. The saddest part of this entire episode hadn't happened yet.

The woman must have been equally taken aback by the expression on my face. She actually offered to show me the apartment anyway. I remember feeling a little apprehensive about entering her house because of her attitude, but I wanted to see the apartment I would never have. Looking back at this incident, it is hard for me to think just how badly I felt about myself to actually agree to take a look at the apartment after what she had said to me, but I did. I think, too, that I was out to prove to her, as I felt I had to prove to everyone else in my life, that I really was a good, honest person.

As we ascended the staircase to the second floor no words passed between us. The first room I entered was a good-sized living room with a beautiful hardwood floor and a large picture window. The kitchen was also a nice size and had a great view. It had plenty of cabinet space and a beautiful tiled floor. The bedroom was small, but would have been large enough for me. I loved the apartment, but I could tell that she was not about to change her mind about renting it to me, and I wondered if she might be dangerous, with such an attitude. I think she showed it to me so I could see what I was going to miss out on. She knew how much I liked it. I loved it! It was perfect for me, not too large or small—perfect! It was the apartment I had dreamed of, but it would remain in my dreams.

As we walked down the stairs to the outside door she asked me if I would give her a ride to downtown Salem. She said she could not afford a taxi. I couldn't believe she was asking me to help her after she had been so nasty to me. Did she even want to be seen with me? Was she going to put a bag over her head until she got to her destination? Perhaps it is more unbelievable that I agreed to assist her. I felt sick inside and very hurt by what she had said, however, I couldn't be mean to her. She needed help and I could help her, and I still was on my mission to prove to her that I wasn't a bad person, despite how I looked to her jaundiced eyes. Why should I be like her, with hate in her heart? However, I knew in my own heart that I was mentally unhealthy. I hurt so deep inside that my heart held only sorrow and my soul cried to her, *Please, give me a chance.* I felt alone and empty again. Would anyone ever give me a chance? Would I ever find a place to live on my own?

Even if she had changed her mind and decided to rent me the apartment, I don't think I would have ever felt safe living in a place where the landlady in residence held so much prejudice and rage. I learned a lot about myself from that experience. I wondered if I was going to experience more prejudice in my further search. I felt the chains of discrimination, but I was determined not to give up. There had to be someone out there that would find me acceptable enough.

I continued my search for the perfect apartment, always wondering if I was being selfish and thinking only of myself for wanting to be on my own. Many different kinds of thoughts ran through my mind. Maybe I deserved to be treated in that way. Maybe that woman's horrible words were a sign from God telling me to stay where I am. My mind and body were screaming for help.

My luck changed. While working at North Shore Community College, a fellow employee named Nancy and I were conversing one day and she mentioned that she was moving out of her apartment in South Hamilton. *Did I want to rent it?* she wondered. Would I have a chance at this opportunity? What would the landlady think when she saw me? My tenacious spirit still wanted to go for it. What did I have to lose? I had already been rejected, so what the heck? I told Nancy that I would indeed be most interested in taking a look at the apartment.

One day during our lunch break we drove to see her apartment. I immediately fell in love with it. It was a basement apartment underneath a lovely ranch house, and it was big! It had five rooms that consisted of a large eat-in kitchen, an even larger living room, two medium-sized bedrooms, and an extra storage room that could be used for an additional room if needed. It was in a beautiful, wooded residential area. Its backyard abutted the famous Myopia Polo Club.

Would I receive the opportunity to rent this beautiful abode? Nancy was moving out shortly so I knew a decision would have to be made fairly soon. I had already made mine: I wanted it! I asked Nancy if she could talk to her landlady and set up an interview. I was nervous and scared after the last one. What would she think when she saw me?

I received a call from the landlady to set up a time when I could meet her and her daughter. I found my way again to the home and rang the bell. She opened the door and I introduced myself. She welcomed me in and introduced me to her daughter Diane. The landlady was a very gracious lady. We talked for a long time and I found out that she had taken courses at North Shore Community College. She was very interested in me and she seemed to like me. She was interested in what I had to say and I shared with her my desire to make it out on my own. I could tell by her demeanor that I had an excellent chance of getting the apartment. She said that she would call me so I gave her my phone numbers at work and at home. I waited, impatiently, but there wasn't anything else I could do. One day I got the call. She liked me and so we sealed the deal, and I had the apartment.

It was time to tell my mom I was moving out. As happy as I was for the move, I had mixed emotions because of the effect I assumed it would have on her. Actually, she was very happy for me and she knew that this is what I had to do. My mom supported me all the way, but still a big part of me felt that I should not move and that I should continue to live with her, to be there for her. I moved into my new apartment with help from my sister Debbie on November 1, 1980. The first month or so I alternated nights, staying at the apartment one night and the next with my mom so she wouldn't be alone. I continued to help her with the expenses but it became very costly for me. I was paying rent at my new abode while still helping my mom. It wasn't long after I moved out that my mom decided to sell the house. She sold it in April of 1981 and started a new life. She rented a townhouse in Peabody and quickly adjusted. In fact she loved being alone. It was a new experience for her because she had gone from her parents' home to married life to bringing up her kids. She was off on her own personal journey.

I think back on this experience of apartment searching and see that it affected my life in many positive ways, and yet it didn't come without a heavy price. Moving out, starting a new relationship, recovering from the ills of cancer, dealing with guilt from my move, and just feeling so badly about myself in every way possible took a heavy toll on my mental health.

I believe the emotional toll of these life-altering events led to my eating disorder. In the end though, moving out on my own was something I needed to do, and it was one of the best decisions I ever made.

17

Starving to be Perfect

It was the summer of 1964 and I was fourteen years old when I decided to go on
a diet. I was finally free from the perils of Catholic school and the bullying and
cruel treatment that I had received while I was there. The cruelty of kids who bullied me left a mark that was so damaging that it stayed imbedded in my being,
but I was out to rid myself of that indelible pain. I was going to make a new start.
I began my mission to gain control of my life by losing weight. A "new me" for
my new adventure into high school was about to emerge. I had ten weeks to
accomplish this task. I was escaping the kids who hated me. I was leaving behind
the nuns who didn't take the time to understand what was going on to protect
me. I was the captain of my own ship, and I was setting sail to a place I had never
been, in search of happiness and acceptance. I was out to prove to the world that
there was a person named Jacqui who really wasn't as bad as how others had
treated her. Dieting was the perfect solution, so I thought.

During that summer I dieted strictly. I felt I was fat and ugly. I knew if I lost
weight there would be a chance for me to find happiness. I felt sure that if I were
thin then maybe I would be accepted. In actuality, at 5' 2" with a medium frame,
my heaviest weight had never been more than over five pounds off the charts.
Technically, I was always within my ideal weight range, but that didn't matter to
me then. I felt fat; therefore, I was fat. I lost fifteen pounds by the end of the summer, without letting much pass through my lips, and was proud of my accom-
plishment. It was a good start, but the dieting never stopped, and I wasn't
satisfied. But then, no matter how hard I tried I could not lose more, or could I?
This would become a lifetime struggle for me, but at the time I was the captain
and I had the control, or so I thought. I needed to try harder; maybe I wasn't trying hard enough. I always had to work for everything I wanted. I never had the
privilege of something coming easy to me, or just having it handed over to me
like so many people I knew; at least it seemed that way.

I never allowed myself even one little cheat. I wouldn't even eat my own birthday cake! I felt if I even took a little bite that I would gain the weight right back. How sad is that? All I thought about was how many calories were in one piece of cake and how much weight I would gain from it. It became my way of life. Pizza was another food I deprived myself of and it had been my very favorite food. I avoided and deprived myself of all of the foods that gave me the most comfort.

I remember one day I helped a friend move out of her apartment. We packed boxes and lifted them into a van to be transported to her new home. We unloaded the van and unpacked the boxes and began to distribute the boxes in their appropriate place. We started to wash cabinets, floors, and anything that needed cleaning. She had ordered pizza for us to eat, not knowing that I wouldn't eat it. Who wouldn't eat pizza? Who doesn't like pizza? It was something quick, but for sure a comfort food. I would not allow myself to even take a bite of the pizza. I believed I didn't deserve to feel good or be comforted. I remember how hungry I was but just munched on a salad and Diet Coke. Looking back, I am sure I burned enough calories to have earned at least one piece of pizza. Even knowing that, I still would not have indulged.

I was staying the same weight—not gaining, but not losing—and I began to hate my body. I hated everything about me. Why was even my own body against me? I looked at it as though some actual *being* was against me. I continued obscure eating patterns for years. I tried all types of diets, none of them healthy. One of my diets consisted of mainly green beans. All I would eat were green beans. An entire cup was only fifteen calories. I bought a calorie book and studied it from cover to cover. I took it everywhere I went. I memorized it. I felt proud that they would ask me the calorie content of a particular food and was happy that I could tell them. I remember feeling how unfair it was when my work friends and I would go out to lunch. They would order pizza and I would order a salad with diet dressing. They never seemed to gain weight but I knew if ever I indulged as they were I would end up looking like Porky Pig.

My behavior eventually grew into a full-blown eating disorder. I was unaware of this at the time, of course; all I knew is that I wanted to be thin. I was on a mission and there was no turning back, even though I also thought I was crying out for help and I felt no one cared even to listen. I lived in my own private hell. The emptiness inside me continued to grow, but it was not from starvation. Why was I cursed with a metabolism that made me gain weight even from eating pickles? I hated my body, and grew so frustrated trying so hard and getting nowhere.

I can't remember exactly when I decided to add purging to my list of self-abusive punishment, but I was an adult and it was my life and my decision. I remember reading in a magazine about eating disorders and how throwing up really didn't have an ill feeling affect on how one felt physically. If I purged right after I ate, my body had not had a chance to digest the food yet so throwing it up immediately left me without that sick feeling one has after throwing up. I could "enjoy" food and not have to pay the price of gaining weight. It sounded ideal to me. I was already an expert on throwing up due to the chemotherapy I had experienced. Hey, if I could throw up for eleven solid hours each of the two days I received chemotherapy what difference would this kind of purging mean? I still would not allow myself to eat pizza.

My eating disorder accelerated then into bulimia. This started just around the time I moved out of the house into my own apartment. I was dating Matt, in a relationship that was very bewildering to me, and I was trying to make a new start. I remember going into the bathroom and sticking my finger down my throat and gagging myself until I threw up. *Hey, that was easy!* I said to myself. I didn't have any nausea and there was no odor of vomit. I never really binged on food, as many bulimics do. I would go to a restaurant and order "dry" fish (no butter), green beans, and salad with diet dressing. The fish was a splurge for me. I was afraid to allow myself butter in case it would somehow creep into my system before I could get rid of it. I was so strict that I limited myself to less than 800 calories a day. This got to be a habit, an everyday ritual. If I dined at a restaurant I visited the bathroom shortly after I ate, waited until no one was there and then emptied my stomach. I loved it when they had a bathroom that was for one only. I would run the water in the sink so no one could hear me purge. I would feel good if I could "eat" for a change, and not have to pay the price. I was finally in control of my body and life, so I thought.

During that time I decided to start an exercise program. I knew with the combination of the two—purging and regular exercise—that I could lose weight. I hated my body and *knew* my body hated me. Exercising soon became an obsession with me. I joined the YMCA and taught myself how to swim. I would go to the Y at 6:00 AM and swim a mile without stopping. I would return after work and exercise another two hours. I went every day, including Saturday and Sunday. I couldn't quit. I needed to do it. I felt in control and very strong. It gave me a high. I felt proud that I was so much in control. Even when my body was exhausted I would ignore its complaints and continue with my regiment. I would not give in to it. This time my body was going to listen to me. Little did I know or even want to believe, it really had control of me.

My entire life and how I felt about myself had always relied upon other's opinions of me. I was hungry for affection. I had tried to be strong long before my emotional and maturational development took place. The little girl in me remained hidden. Emotionally I felt like a child whose favorite doll had been taken away and ripped into pieces in front of her. I was always on the verge of tears. It took very little for me to feel hurt. I grew up believing that I should not be demanding of others. I had no right to *want*. I felt no self worth and had an extreme need for the approval of others. I never felt I was doing the right thing. I always felt I was doing something wrong. If I did something right, it was just adequate and I should try even harder. Everyone was always better than me. No matter how hard I tried, someone was always better, and I was made aware of it. If I even suggested or tried to suggest that I did a good job, I was torn apart for it. *Who do you think* you *are?* Looking back, I realize I probably sabotaged myself because I never fought back, but I believed that if I fought back they might feel hurt by what I had to say. I did not want to inflict any pain on anyone. I knew how it felt and I just couldn't fight back in that manner. I was like a wounded bird in the middle of a field of stray cats.

I starved myself to be below the charts. The scale was my enemy. I weighed myself daily. My time was consumed with how I was going to get rid of calories and when. I knew what I could allow myself to eat and what all the "forbidden fruits" were. I constantly asked myself, *if only, if only*, as in, *If only I could just lose the weight I might be noticed in some positive way.* I hated my life and I hated me.

I can never explain the deep emptiness that I felt at that time well enough. I was wretched and so lonely. I continued my search. Later in life I found a few interesting facts about people who suffer from an eating disorder. One of them was that often people who suffer eating disorders are anxious and conflicted about leaving the home. I was. However, it was more than that and so much deeper, but I do believe the event of moving out put the wheels of my eating disorder into motion. As I was contemplating getting my own apartment I felt guilty about leaving my mother alone.

Another fact is that sufferers of eating disorders might have played an important role in their family. I was a person who took over for someone who was no longer visible or available when needed, I took the place of my dad leaving home; I also took the place, in some ways, of my dead brother and my sisters who'd left to start their own families. Once again my mom would be abandoned, but this time it would be me who left her. How could I? How would I dare allow myself to leave? I had spent all my time helping and protecting my mother. She was my greatest concern. I needed me to protect her. She deserved to have happiness. I tried to make up to her what my father took away. I wanted to take away her pain. She had to be happy before I deserved to be happy. I could hardly concentrate on my own feelings.

I needed to feed the hole within me. I was very despondent and very sad. I had been emotionally abused and traumatized as a child at school and in my neighborhood and had no say or control over my life. I had been bullied continuously. I thought that getting full control over my body was one way I could take control of what happened to me. But I related to the words of the Neil Diamond song, "I have emptiness deep inside and it won't let me go."

Eventually, I was tired of feeling so empty and living on empty, and I never let go of the thread of hope. I knew I didn't want to live this way forever. I decided to seek counseling. After much counseling and soul searching, I understood that this destructive behavior was not the answer. Today I rarely think about purging, yet I must say that I still continue to watch my weight carefully, I just do it in a more positive way. I am still careful in what I eat, but I allow myself to indulge now and then. Food doesn't control my life anymore, and I am more accepting of my body. I still exercise almost daily, but not excessively. I realize I will never be perfect and that's okay. This realization was a giant step for me.

18

The Dating Company

I was so tired of the regular club scene. It was always the same old thing. Going clubbing never really worked for me, although I really did try to enjoy it. Week after week, my girlfriends and I would try different clubs along the North Shore area. There were many clubs to choose from and all different types of music at them, from country western to disco to jazz to sixties music, and everything in between. Music was my lifeline. I loved popular music. It was the seventies and I loved the music of the times. I enjoyed listening to the Beatles, Neil Diamond, Beach Boys, the Carpenters, the Mamas and the Papas, Fleetwood Mac, the Everly Brothers, the Righteous Brothers, Credence Clearwater Revival, the Moody Blues, et cetera. I just loved music and music was here to stay. I was definitely a "radio" girl.

However, I hated the fact that a woman rarely would ask a guy to dance back then; rather, she had to wait for a guy to ask her to dance. I didn't feel very popular at the club scene. Looking back, I believe that I gave off vibes that I was unapproachable. I was scared of rejection. I felt from the start that no one was going to ask me to dance and very few did. I felt rejected and probably projected that. I tried to be nonchalant, but the fact that I was trying so hard made it worse. It became too much of an effort. I really wasn't having a good time. I wasn't sure whether or not I really wanted to even be there most nights because, except for the great music, I really didn't have all that much fun. I was usually the one sitting there while my friends were up dancing. This did a job on my bruised ego.

I remember dressing up really nicely with makeup and in stylish clothes. Even so, I had this complex that any eligible bachelors were shying away from me because they liked the *pretty, shapely, light-skinned* girls. Still, I felt that at least I had to make the attempt to meet someone. Then I could never say that I didn't try. So I continued my weekly ritual of going out to clubs every Friday and Saturday evening in hopes that maybe, just maybe, I would get lucky.

I even ventured out on my own. This was totally not me. I got all dressed up and went to a nightclub early so I would not have to walk into a large crowd. The crowd would walk in when I was already there. I sat up at the bar and talked to the bartender when he wasn't busy. I remember one particular time I was sitting at the bar and a young gentleman sent over a drink to me. I didn't know what to do. I shyly looked at him with a slight thank you and looked away. I felt very uncomfortable. I thought it might be some cruel joke he was playing on me. Clubbing clearly wasn't for me, but what else could I do? I certainly didn't want to stay home alone on a Friday or Saturday night.

One evening I was listening to a radio program on a local station, and the topic was "dating." A representative of a dating service explained what his company was all about. He owned the company and it was new, so he was on the air to promote it. I liked his voice, which is what caught my attention. I wanted to know more about his company. I remember thinking that it must be safe and reputable if a radio station was sponsoring it, especially since it was one of the most popular radio stations in the Boston area. I was excited that this might be a new way to meet someone. It was worth listening to what he had to say if nothing else. The more I listened, the more excited I got. It really sounded great.

He explained that the way the dating service worked was that a client would participate in a videotaped interview. The room was like a television studio and an interviewer would ask the client questions regarding likes, dislikes, and the types of people he or she would be interested in meeting. There were no right or wrong answers. It all depended on what the interviewee was looking for in a relationship. It was done in a very professional manner and was on the level. I had a good feeling about it. I telephoned one of my girlfriends to see if she would be interested in exploring this adventure with me. She was. We called the service's number and spoke to the receptionist. I remember her abundant enthusiasm. We made an appointment and headed into Boston.

My friend and I were both impressed with the detailed information we received and the great tour of the studio. We continued to be interested. We signed up and made another appointment to come in for our taping of our own personal videos. We returned to the studio and my friend and I were each videotaped. It was an exciting day for us. This seemed the perfect way to meet someone without any hassle. In any event, it was a lot of fun. We couldn't wait until we started getting our dates. We couldn't help but think how the men would view us, or if we would get any calls at all. We were also excited about viewing their tapes, too.

It worked, and went like this: after someone viewed my tape the dating service sent a postcard that stated, "Someone has seen your tape and would like you to see theirs." If I was interested, I called for an appointment to see the person's tape, and if I was interested in meeting this person they gave me his name and number and sent him my name and phone number. The next step was to wait for a call, or if I was inclined I could call him. As expected, some would call and some would not, for whatever reasons they may have had. This was quite different than anything I had ever experienced. It was also a way of meeting someone who had seen me on tape before actually meeting me.

I really enjoyed my membership in the dating service because I did not have to put up with all the hassles of clubs. I could be selective, because I got to decide whether or not to make contact. It was a really positive way of meeting people. I never thought I would find myself doing something such as this, but I love adventure and I am glad I tried it. It was fun waiting for the mail and seeing a dating service card waiting for me in the mailbox. I had been with the service for only three months and I had seen many tapes. It was great for my ego, especially since the gentlemen had seen what I looked like. They wouldn't be surprised or disappointed when they saw me because they already had viewed my tape. I could choose the tapes I wanted to see and decide what I wanted to do next. There was absolutely no pressure. The cost was only fifteen dollars for a six-month membership, and could be renewed for the same price. This was a great price, even then. No more clubs. It was perfect.

Little did I know that this spur-of-the-moment decision to venture out on a new experience would end up lasting twelve years. It was through this service that I met Matt. It all began with a phone call one evening. *Hello, is Jacqui there? This is Matt.* On the evening of April 9, 1977, we had our first date, a date that lasted twelve years.

19

Matt

I remember the phone call as it if were yesterday. I answered the phone and a calming voice asked to speak to Jacqui. I absolutely loved his voice. He told me he was calling as a member of the dating service, and that his name was Matt. I think we must have spoken for two hours that first night. We talked about family, our work, and our lives. We hit it off just fine, and we made a date to meet. I was excited and anxious at the same time.

Our first date was April 9, 1977. I liked Matt from the start. He was warm, sensitive, and extremely kind. He told me how he had intended to become a priest and had gone to a seminary high school. The school had a difficult and challenging curriculum. While there, a priest befriended Matt and suggested that he should seek another career. Matt never explained exactly why the priest counseled him in this way, but as I grew to know Matt better I understood that Matt would not have been able to take the emotional stress of what is often required of the priesthood. Instead, Matt graduated from high school and entered the navy.

He shared many of his stories about navy life with me. While Matt was in the service and stationed in Hong Kong, he met a woman with whom he fell in love and they became engaged. He gave her a beautiful diamond ring. Matt returned to the States after completing his duty in the navy with all intentions of sending for his love. They had stayed in touch through letters and phone calls for three months, when he received a very disturbing call. His love had been killed in a car accident. He was devastated. Years had passed and Matt said he dated many women, but found he could never really connect with any of them in the way he needed to. He was still searching for someone to love again, and right from the start when we met he felt that I was the one. I, on the other hand, had a trust issue and a deep inner gut feeling that something wasn't right. I didn't know what it was or if I was just looking for something flawed, as was my usual way. I liked Matt enough, though, so that I decided to take my time and try not to predict any kind of outcome.

I quickly found out that Matt was a person who needed nurturing. I was good at that. This fit into my profile as a caretaker, perfectly. I was a caretaker again, and it seemed to be all I knew how to do. Again, as I had done in previous relationships, I chose a man who I felt was safe. I didn't feel threatened by these men because I never felt they could devastate-me when they left my life. I picked men who would be good to me, and in return I would be good to them. I might love them, but I knew deep in my heart and soul that I would never allow myself to be *in love* with them. When I lost a man I was in love with, I knew, it would be too much pain for me to bear. In choosing to go this route I could still have relationships with men like Matt and at the same time spare myself from any pain. This was all part of my control and defense mechanism of keeping safe. The only problem is that I sabotaged myself. I still wanted to *want* to get married. It left me feeling confused and frustrated because I couldn't make myself feel this way.

Matt was so terrific to me. What was the matter with me? It was so difficult to be openly honest. I didn't want to hurt him. But still, as I had done with Brian and Chris before him, I told Matt of my feelings of not knowing if I could ever trust or love someone in a way that one should love, for a lasting relationship. And, as the others had also done, he said would give me as much time as I needed. Although I thought that the time required might just be forever, he insisted it didn't matter, that he would wait, and so I agreed to continue seeing him. I am sure, as the others had thought in times past, that he thought I would change my mind. We broke up four times in our twelve-year relationship but he always wooed me back. All the times I went back I had hope I could change and feel the trust, but it never totally happened. This was very upsetting for both of us. Matt had the patience of Job, but mine was wearing thin. What was the matter with me?

The first time we broke up was four months into our relationship. I didn't want to hurt Matt and already I knew at that point he wanted to marry me and that I couldn't say yes. I felt it wasn't fair to him. Breaking up with Matt did not go too well, but we did separate for three months. I received cards from Matt every week. He started to call me, not in a harassing way, but pleading to give him another chance. Some mornings I would find a card and a dollar for a cup of coffee inside the envelope on my car's windshield. He missed me and he wanted me back. He would do anything if I would give him another chance. I did. But he wasn't doing anything wrong, and nothing promised to change for me.

As much as Matt loved and cared for me, it was a very emotionally draining relationship because I couldn't change the way things were. We had many differences; not in values this time, but in how we lived our everyday lives. I tried desperately to adjust my world to fit his world, but to no avail. I blamed myself for being selfish and for not being able to change. I had a man who wanted to give me the world, and just about did, but I was unable to reciprocate. I wanted to, but couldn't. I loved him in a special way, but not in the way that mattered for what he wanted.

Perhaps I knew the answer, a very simple answer, but I didn't want to face it. I resented my father and blamed him for instilling in me the total lack of trust that I still carry with me today. I had to forgive my father in order to regain the capacity for trust. I tried relentlessly to change the way I felt. It wasn't as though I didn't want to be loved, held, kissed, and made love to—I craved that affection—it was just that I couldn't trust that if I completely gave myself over to the man who provided it that he wouldn't just abandon me as soon as I had, crippling me forever. I craved for someone who actually loved me, for me. I needed it, wanted it, and I would not give up, even as I knew it wouldn't last because I wouldn't let it. Matt gave it all to me, and more. He loved me. I was sure that he loved me with every beat of his heart. In fact, Matt adored me. I was his world. He treated me like gold.

Matt actually kept a journal of every date we ever had. At the beginning we started going out once a week, and then twice a week, and then three times a week. Imagine the time and energy that went into this journal. Remember, we *dated* for twelve years! Our relationship slowly continued to grow. I was always as honest as I could be with Matt and explained why I could not feel as strong as he did. I could not tell him I loved him when he did. It would take me a lot longer. He had to know this. I told him that if he wanted to continue to see me he would have to be patient and I could hold no promises. He—was willing to wait; he wanted me for as long as it would take. I loved being with him. I had all the attention I craved. We did everything together. We traveled across the country, dined out, went to concerts, took long walks on beaches, went to church and family gatherings together, and spent endless time just being together. I felt fulfilled as a woman. I felt wanted, and it was all because of Matt. But at the same time, I felt miserable. I constantly lived with the guilt that I would probably never be able to commit to Matt in the bond of marriage. I wasn't going to give up trying, though, either. It was too hard, given all that he did for me.

Matt kept telling me that my lack of commitment to him didn't matter, but I knew it did. I knew he wanted to marry me and he was giving me as much time as I needed, but weeks turned into months, months turned into years, and years turned into a decade, and then some. I still hoped, and he still believed I would change my mind.

Matt wanted to give me a ring. I accepted it because I was so tired of always refusing him and perhaps if I made at least this much of a symbolic commitment it would make me realize that this was the right thing to do, but it only confused me more. I wanted to feel like he did so badly. I wanted to want to get married, but I just couldn't catch that elusive butterfly. I loved him and his goodness but I could not love him like I needed to. We set a date for the wedding April ninth, twelve years later on the anniversary of the date we met. I started to make plans. He left all of the plans up to me. I continued to hope that my feelings would change. I prayed and made novenas.

Matt wanted to be a homeowner. He found a condex (one of two condo units in a single house) that he loved. He needed a co-signer and asked me if I would like to be part-owner with him. I agreed. After all, we were getting married. I think we both thought that owning a home together might help bond us even more. It *was* beautiful. It had just been built and we were able to choose the color, decor, carpeting, and fixtures to put in it. We had a great time decorating, picking out shades and curtains, and outfitting the house with furniture from my apartment and from his. It was like we were married and were simply enjoying our new home. But I made-believe this was true. I never did move into the condex but I stayed there on weekends and enjoyed our "married life." I could make believe because I wasn't really married yet. The thought of our actual union, though, spread terror throughout me. Would Matt ever change and become my tormentor? I couldn't imagine it, but that possibility still burned in my mind morning, noon, and even while I slept. Was this a sign or a message? Did I have to get struck by lightning before the light dawned?

There is a song Tammy Wynette sings titled *I Don't Want to Play House* that always played in my head. It tells a story about two children playing together. The little boy asks the little girl if she would like to play house. The little girl begins to cry and tells the little boy that she doesn't want to play house. She tells him that when her mommy played house her daddy went away.

I continued to pray and make novenas, asking my brother and all my friends in heaven to please, please give me a sign. I begged God to help me not be so confused. I don't think I was listening to Him, because I believe now that He was answering me all along. He was letting me be confused and frustrated because the relationship with Matt just wasn't right. I think I didn't want to believe it. I wanted it to be different, and yet at the same time I didn't, because it wasn't. But, Matt and I were no longer in our twenties and I told Matt we had to make some final decisions. This could go on forever. I couldn't take it any longer. We had to take a break, at the very least.

I needed to go somewhere where we would not be tempted to see each other. I decided to fulfill a promise I had made to myself long ago. It was September of 1989 when I told Matt I was going to Lourdes. People of the faith make pilgrimages to Lourdes, France, and it was my time to do so. Many miracles have been granted. I needed to find some answers, and I was fulfilling a promise I made to the Blessed Mother of God that if she would give me strength through my cancer I would thank her by going to Lourdes. I told Matt that this would be a good time for both of us to reflect and take some time for ourselves. We desperately needed time apart.

Everything inside the gates of Lourdes was beautiful. The large cathedral there displayed thousands of crutches that people had left behind as remembrances of the miracles that had occurred. Wheelchairs lay up against the walls of the cathedral and people hoping for a miracle crawled from them on their knees up the long aisle that led to the ornate altar. Beautiful choir voices chanted the beautiful hymns of Our Lady of Lourdes, and the aura of the entire cathedral brought chills to my spine. The grounds of Lourdes were graced with beautiful flowers that led to the miraculous spring where Our Lady of Lourdes had visited the legendary Bernadette. A beautiful peace came over me while I was there, and I felt exceptionally blessed and fortunate that I was able to fulfill my promise. I left my petitions along with others who had given them to me at our Blessed Mother's feet at the shrine.

When I returned from France, Matt told me he had met someone through a dating service and was dating her. I couldn't believe this could happen so quickly. Yet, I could also understand him. So many years had passed by for us, and we still weren't married. I think he was lonely, and perhaps called the service just on a whim. He met someone who was ready to move fast, and he became caught up in the moment.

I felt he never grieved over me, or perhaps he was grieving the entire time we dated. Maybe he had decided that he had waited long enough and he knew, too, finally, that nothing was going to change. I was happy for him but yet I couldn't help feeling so betrayed. I knew that our time apart and our break up this time was to be the last. It was obvious to me that he had found a woman who was willing to marry him. This is what he had wanted all along. I couldn't give him that final commitment so he had sought and found it elsewhere. I couldn't blame him, but I couldn't understand how he could make such a quick decision. Nine months later Matt was married to his new love. Matt actually asked me to attend their September wedding. This was Matt still including me in his life. I did not attend.

One Saturday morning the following October I was in Dunkin Donuts having coffee alone when Matt appeared. He had pictures of his wedding right there with him, which he showed me. Again, this was Matt. He did not do this to be cruel, but to include me in his happy event. It wasn't until years later that Matt and I agreed to have my name taken off the deed and mortgage on the home we had bought together. I guess we both still hung on to a thread that still bonded us together in some strange way.

As before with other men, I know I made the right decision with Matt. I saw, too, that if I have been more honest with myself, I would have made a decision sooner. It would have been kinder to Matt to let him go earlier, but I always hung on to the hope that just maybe it would work. I thought I would hurt him by leaving him, but it would have been the better decision.

I will always have a special place in my heart for Matt. He gave me life when I felt dead. He loved me more than I could ever imagine anyone could. He helped me live the years I lost through my traumas of adolescence. I experienced life like I never would have if it weren't for him. For all of this I am forever grateful to him, and I will always love him.

20

Friends

Tina—my friend who stuck by me

My mom always told us, *"Remember, kids, you're your own best friend."* This is one of the most important things I learned from her. Through the years I found out she was absolutely right. It was a painful lesson for me, but of course I had to learn the hard way and find out for myself. I am not saying that I haven't found true friendship along the way, because indeed I have. In order to have true friends you need to be a true friend. For me, friends are those who don't care what others think and don't feel they have to choose sides. These are people who I can talk to because I know they understand me. They do not criticize and do not judge. They like me for who I am. They accept me despite my shortcomings. I can be myself with them. I can cry, laugh, and sing (even if I can't carry a tune in a bucket), and they like me anyway. I can tell them how I feel knowing that they will understand. Friends are people I know I can be with in a group, and when I walk away they aren't talking negatively about me. Friends are those from whom I feel positive energy when I am around them. I can't see it, but I can certainly feel it.

It was only after I graduated from high school that I began to form lasting friendships, other than my life-long friend, Tina. Although I was very cautious, I allowed myself to take the risk on certain people, in hopes that among them I could find a friend that liked me for me. Every time I got close to someone, though, I could still feel that the emptiness still had a hold on me, which bothered me. I guess I thought if my friendships were full enough, then that void would be filled, too. Something was missing in my life, and no matter how hard I tried to find out what it was, it always seemed to elude me. I was happy on the surface to have friends, but beneath it all I was still crying and had to continue my search to find the missing piece of the puzzle. With each and every friendship came comfort, but it wasn't enough.

As I grew emotionally healthier I made greater friendships. I decided to share some of my experiences that I'd had with dear friends. I had to learn to first be a friend to myself, and only then did I allow friends into my life without the fear of being hurt. I feel this is one of the most important chapters in my book because learning to have friends is a great triumph for me. I never thought I would have any friends and I now have many. They are an important part of my life and they have contributed very much to my healing. The experiences we share together have helped me grow into the person I am today.

Tina was my first true friend. She was there for me in the darkest moments of my life. I am eternally grateful to her. We have been friends since childhood. She lived across the street from me and we went to the same schools together. She was five and I was six when we met. She was one year behind me in school. I will forever be thankful to God for putting her into my life. She remained my friend through my hellish years of grammar school. She was my friend, and she didn't care if no one else was. She didn't care if the bullies didn't like her because she liked me. We weren't able to be together very much in school because she was in a different grade and was on a different schedule, but when we did pass each other she always acknowledged me with a smile. We bonded and still remain friends.

Tina would often stay at my house. My mom loved Tina like her own daughters and let Tina join us on our Sunday rides. She frequently joined us for supper, too. Tina always wanted to be with us. We were like sisters. Every Saturday we walked to a diner down the street from where we lived and treated ourselves to nice juicy hamburgers and French fries or onion rings. This was prior to my "crazy diet phase."

Christine

Tina in my backyard

We both held sadness in our hearts but we managed to laugh and play. We played in my backyard and swung on the double swings until our hearts were content and until the next time we were together. We also had quiet times when we didn't say anything at all but were simply there for each other. We loved each other and we were best friends. She was also my only friend, then.

Neither of us knew then how we were each other's savior. I didn't know much about the pain Tina faced everyday, and she didn't know all that I went through, but we both knew about the bullies in our neighborhood and at school. I remember walking down the street with Tina and the bullies harassed and bulled me as we passed them, but I had Tina by my side and together we tried to ignore them and continued walking to wherever we were going. These encounters never stopped my friend from being just that, a friend.

Tina's home life was filled with turmoil. She felt insecure in her surroundings and she longed for a mother like mine. I, on the other hand, wished for a dad like hers. I knew very little about him but he came home every night, and that was enough for me. We made our own little corner of our own little world. When we were together, we had the sense of a place of escape where we didn't have to say anything to know we were there for each other. We sang hymns we learned in Catholic school and songs of praise to our Blessed Mother. We sang songs from the radio and made-believe we were stars. We found peace and solitude with each other.

During high school we didn't hang around with each other as much. Tina was into dating and I was bound and determined to get control and find a new life for myself. When we graduated from high school we continued down different paths. Tina got married and had a child. Her husband was in the service at the time and she moved to Germany. We wrote for a while, but somehow lost touch. It wasn't until I discovered serendipitously that a colleague of mine had worked with Tina at a local hospital that I found my old friend again. She arranged for the three of us to meet. It was a great reunion. I felt like we had never been apart. We made a promise to each other that we would continue to see each other as we had so very long ago. We felt the same bond then that we had as kids. Now we get together often and always reminisce about our lives as children and how very much we were each other's anchors. I thank Donna for bringing us together again after all these years.

My closest friend after Tina was Marilyn, who I met when we were both nineteen years old. We met while she and I was working at the state school for the developmentally disabled. We liked each other from the start. We were both quiet, yet we felt like we had always known each other. I knew she was a nice person from the moment I met her. I knew I had found a friend. Marilyn was kind, gentle, and sincere. She had a mom and dad, one sister, and four brothers. Her family reminded me of my own. They loved each other and they all pitched in as a family to survive their ordeals. I connected with her and felt in my heart that she was a true friend. She liked me despite how I felt about myself. I was so grateful to her and knew in my heart that she was a keeper.

Even after I left the position at the state school, Marilyn and I continued our friendship. We don't see each other often today, but we still have a strong friendship. We talk to each other at least once a week and we are there for each other. I know that I could call Marilyn at 3:00 AM and she would be there for me, no questions asked. We lead different lives but we share similar values and concerns. We have both had losses and have been there for each other and always will be. I am very thankful to have her in my life. I know she feels the same about me. What more could one ask for?

I met Kathy on a plane while traveling to see my sister and her husband who was stationed in New Jersey. We connected right away and talked the entire trip about our jobs, families, and friends. We both knew we wanted to be friends with each other well beyond the plane trip. She told me all about Cape Cod, and how beautiful it was in the summer months. She invited me to spend a weekend with her and her family when the summer arrived. We exchanged phone numbers. I couldn't wait, and I did take her up on her offer. I was totally blown away by the beauty of that part of Massachusetts. I had never explored it, and found paradise. Through the years onward, Kathy and I shared many good times. Life led us along different paths and we didn't see each other for long stretches of time, but we always kept in touch. We never lost the deep connection that we have to this very day. Our friendship was meant to be.

I first met Carolyn when she was working part time at the college where we were both employed. She has been my confidante. I have felt comfortable sharing many childhood experiences with her. She has been able to share her own personal experiences with me, too, and together we have helped each other. I liked her from the very start. Her true spirit shines through everything she does, and she is warm, caring, and non-judgmental. She never has a bad word to say about anyone. She, like me, sees the good in each and every person that she meets, and she wasn't afraid to be my friend.

One of my most memorable experiences with Carolyn happened while attending a seminar in Hollywood, Florida. It was a three-day conference titled "The Heart of Happiness." It was one of the most rewarding experiences that I have ever had. We went to a session featuring James Van Praagh, a renowned psychic. He was absolutely wonderful. I hoped that perhaps my brother or grandmother would come through to him, but, alas, they didn't. However, the people he did reach enriched my life and I felt a piece of heaven. These people were related to other people in the group, and not to me, but I was convinced by the experience that I would somehow meet those in my life who has passed on someday. I know they are happy and would most likely never choose to return here on earth but I also believe that they will greet me with open arms when I encounter them. I bought Mr. Praagh's three books and he kindly autographed them for me. I feel he is truly blessed and has been given a special gift from God Almighty. He believes in God, and often mentioned Him in his connection with life beyond. I came away from there feeling filled with the Holy Spirit. I so appreciate Carolyn as the woman she is, for going with me to that conference, and for the wonderful friendship that we share.

Jennifer and I met in graduate school. It is funny how things happen. I was taking one of my last few courses before I graduated, and Jennifer joined the class late as a last option. The course was called Community Counseling. The professor started the class with an icebreaker game. The object of the game was for all the students to form a straight line in the correct order of their birth month and day without speaking to one another. We could use gestures, but no verbal language. So the game began. My birthday is September 30 and so is Jennifer's. As we wound our way through the line of our classmates nonverbally, we approached each other with humor. It was quite comical when we both fought for the last space in the ninth month section of the line. It finally dawned on us that we had the same birthday. It turned out that we had more in common than our birthday.

I loved Jennifer from the start. I loved her smile, her kindness, and her humor. She possessed a way about her that shined like a queen's diamond crown. She indeed sparkled. We sat across from each other in class and got to know each other a little better. Soon, I felt like I had always known her. As I listened to her talk about her difficulty obtaining an internship (through no fault of her own), I wanted to help and hoped that what I was going to suggest would turn out to be a positive step for her. I was working at the Student Support Center at North Shore Community College and I knew that we accepted interns from various colleges. I thought Jennifer would be a perfect intern. She had the personality, and she was smart. I asked Jennifer if she would be interested in working at the college in our center and she gratefully agreed. I spoke to my supervisor the next morning about Jennifer. My friend had an excellent resume, and my supervisor agreed to meet with her. Jennifer was offered and accepted the internship. She continued to succeed and gained much knowledge in various areas of the college. She eventually obtained a full-time position at the college.

We had in common very strong bonds with our mothers. We often talked about this and how we both were caretakers of our moms. We both felt responsible for their well-being and happiness. We each had taken over the "husband" role, and believed it was most important that our mothers were well cared for and happy. This had been a huge burden for us as children and it continued into our adulthood. Unfortunately, Jennifer's mom passed away in 2002. My heart went out to her. I could not imagine her pain. I cannot even think about my own mom passing away. I don't feel I could survive her loss. However, I learned a lot from Jennifer through her painful experience. We both lost our dads at a very early age. Jennifer lost hers through death and I lost mine through a living death. We both shared the feelings of those who grow up without a dad. We shared how we missed them and how it might have been or could have been.

Jennifer and I think very much the same way. Sometimes this can be detrimental to us. Often we put others before ourselves. It is important that we don't offend anyone, even if they are offending us, because we know how it feels. We sacrifice our own feelings for fear of hurting others. We cannot comprehend how people can be so inconsiderate and nasty sometimes.

Today I feel our friendship is stronger than ever. Although we are very much alike in many ways, we are still our individual selves. We respect each other and do not take advantage of our friendship. We are open and honest with each other. I treasure her friendship and I only hope that I am as much of a friend to her as she is to me. She is a true friend.

Nancy has been my friend for many years, and although we lead different lives we have always kept it a priority to keep in touch and see each other regularly. She has a wonderful husband Paul and two wonderful daughters, Jennifer and Kate. She has had own her share of sorrow and pain. She is a cancer survivor, too, and with the help and support of her family and friends she was able to fight the horrible disease with courage and dignity. It was a battle, but she made it. We share that experience, and we share memories of our "cruise" to Nova Scotia and trip to New Brunswick, Canada. We care very much about each other and are always willing to listen to one another, including when we feel like venting. Our friendship is important to us, and is something we both treasure and of which we will never let go.

Joyce, who I met at the college, is a good, caring friend. Although she has since left the college we have kept in touch and see each other often, but not often enough. We still talk on the phone to keep up with what is going on in each of our lives. Each holiday season, Joyce and I organized a successful holiday get-together. It was a lot of work, but we got to do it together and we had a lot of help from various offices that contributed their trademark dishes. It was always a big success.

Joyce has a wonderful family and is able to enjoy and spend more time with them now that she is retired. We manage to travel, now and then, and have seen great parts of this beautiful country together. She likes to travel as much as I do, and we take every opportunity we can to make it happen! I always look forward for us to get together.

Lynne is a dear friend who I met in graduate school. I have shared many fun times with her throughout the years. She is very bright and is a psychiatric nurse at a local mental health agency. She is not only a good friend, but is also a fun friend. We have a tradition every October around Halloween to meet in Salem for the Haunted Happenings. Salem, Massachusetts, is known as the "Witch City" because of the infamous witch trials in the sixteen hundreds, but it has much more history than just that. It is also a "must see" place because of its beautiful Atlantic Ocean seashore and its architectural history. There is so much to see and do in Salem and it is so much fun. Literally thousands of people share in the exciting October events. During the Haunted Happenings, tours pass through the city's old cemeteries where it just might be possible to catch a glimpse of a ghost. Vendors galore pace the pedestrian streets with their craft. Sidewalk musicians entertain the throngs of people. Fortunetellers guarantee their forecasts for a price. It is truly exciting, and Lynne is always as enthusiastic about Salem in October as I am. What a good friend! Being a real family person, she is also dedicated to hers and is very close to her mom and dad. She has shared many things with me in confidence and our friendship continues to grow today.

Barbara is another dear friend of mine. We have been friends for quite a long time. She is also a great listener. She is very compassionate. She works at the college, too, and she works in the same building as my office so it is easy to see her. We are great traveling buddies. At least once a year we travel to Connecticut and go to either the Foxwoods or Mohegan Sun casino for an overnight stay. We are not big gamblers but we do set aside a certain amount of "entertainment money" that we allow ourselves to play with. We spend the rest of the time at the spa enjoying the swimming pool, sauna, and jacuzzi, making believe we are the "Queens of Sheba." We also shop together at the exquisite shops and enjoy the casino's wonderful buffets. It's fun making-believe as adults with Barbara. We are able to share with each other our good times and bad, too.

Donna V. has had some very trying times in her life, but she has managed to pull through them by the grace of God. We have been friends for a long time, with much in common. She also has a lot of faith and is very dedicated to her family. We make it a point to see each other as often as we can. Our sisters are also friends so we often meet with our moms for get-together potluck dinners.

I met Ellyn in graduate school and formed a friendship with her that has lasted for years. It is very easy to see that she and I share a true friendship. I know she genuinely cares about our relationship and that it means a lot to her. She has a beautiful home that she shares with her husband Greg. He is an absolute peach; a gentleman and a dear friend. She trusts me to care for their precious kitties when they're away, and appreciates what I can do for her. Ellyn is kind and considerate of all those around her, and I feel blessed to have her in my life.

Anne is not only a friend but also an "angel on earth." It is very difficult to write just a few lines about Anne, because she possesses a quality that very few people have. I have never known Anne to be less than kind and giving. Her generosity and caring for others is evident in everything she says and does. We met at the college, and were immediately attracted to each other. Her warmth was magnetic and I could not help but be drawn to her. Her positive energy radiates from her like a burst of sunshine. She has a wonderful, caring husband named Joe with whom she shares her life. She never fails to share her warmth. She is a genuine person and my true friend. She is a Reiki master and performs treatments that calm and soothe. We see each other as often as we can and we treasure each moment we are able to share. We are very much alike in many ways, and we have a special understanding about what makes each of us tick. I believe she hides her wings.

Cindy and Kerry are two other dear friends of mine. Each one of these friends has given me the gift of their friendship. I could not ask for more. We make vow to each other that each time we get together we set a date to meet again. We have shared many stories and thoughts with each other. We enjoy each other's company and we don't take each other for granted.

Donna W. is a caring and giving friend who is always willing to lend a helping hand. We volunteer at a homeless shelter together. She does the shopping for the morning breakfast. She is a great friend to me, and I feel we will always remain close. Her warm spirit is her guiding light.

My friends, Judy, Sandy, Ellen, Jean, and Jackie are never to be forgotten. They have always supported me. They are always willing to listen, and they do so with compassion. They are always there for me. I wish we could get together more often over relaxing dinners or similar leisurely activities. I am so fortunate to have them in my life and truly treasure each of them as my friends.

I am grateful to my lunch buddies Joan H., Claudette, Cathy, Karen, and especially Joan P., who helped me get started on this book of mine.

I learned a lot about myself through each of these friendships. I learned that it is not necessary for everyone to like me, but that it is important to have some positive, honest people in my life. I learned that I shouldn't try to be a peacemaker between friends because sometimes it can backfire. Many of my friends have moved on with their lives, but every one of these friendships has enriched my life. My friends will be forever in my heart.

God Bless you all.

Joan, Irene, Dawn, Joyce, Joan, Kathy, Claudette, Jacqui, Marianne +
Joanne-Christmas Party

21

Making a Difference

Throughout my life I have always wanted to make a difference in people's lives. It was one of my missions to find out how I could do this. I found there were endless ways to help those less fortunate than I am. I wanted to give them hope and I wanted to give something back. I wanted to see a person who may never have smiled find some joy in his or her heart.

I applied to VISTA (Volunteers in Service to America) in 1969. Unfortunately, they required their volunteers to have a minimum of an associate's degree from an accredited college. I felt badly that I would not be able to pursue my goal through this great service because I lacked a higher education degree, but I was determined to find another way to help the less fortunate. At the time it never occurred to me to go to college and get my degree. Back then, I was always led to believe that I wasn't college material.

It was at this time that I applied at the state school for children with developmental disabilities, which happened to be located just about a mile from my house. I had seen that a position was open there, and had an interview with a woman named Phyllis. She was very nice and seemed interested in me. To my surprise I got the position. as a program aide. I was assigned my own classroom and would be working with six children. The children were severely developmentally delayed and also had multiple handicaps, such as cerebral palsy, blindness, hearing loss, and psychotic disabilities. While no higher education was required of me at the state school, in-service educational classes were offered on site and free of charge for the staff. The classes helped educate us about how to handle the children and deal with issues that might arise with them.

It was at the state school that I met my dear friend Marilyn, and together we planned programs for the children. The children's ages ranged from six to ten years old, but they had mental capacities of anywhere from nine months to two years. I worked with a physical therapist who assisted the children with exercises that strengthened their leg and arm muscles to keep them from atrophying. I continued the exercises with each child on a daily basis. I also worked with an occupational therapist who helped the children learn basic, daily living skills, such as how to hold a spoon so they could feed themselves. We then practiced these skills everyday. A music therapist visited the children on a weekly basis and brought in different musical instruments that she played for the children. Each child had the opportunity to feel or stroke the instrument and listen to the different sounds that each instrument produced. During the week, I improvised with a wooden spoon and a pan for a drum, or a small keyboard for a piano. The children thrived with these types of therapy, which produced lots of smiles and laughter. They truly loved music time. Each child seemed to have an awakening when listening to music.

It lifted my spirit to see the spirit of the children lifted as high as a bird could fly. I loved my job. I acquired knowledge, which aided me in acquiring the skills I needed to help the children reach their highest potential. The children in my group really progressed. They were severely handicapped, yet they were able to reach heights that were thought of them to be unattainable. All but one child learned to feed himself, and one child learned to walk on his own for the first time ever. All of them loved music and they all felt loved.

I truly fell in love with these kids. I remember asking my mom if I could bring them to our home for their birthdays and such. She agreed, and so they each had their own private birthday party with balloons, birthday cake, and of course, gifts galore. The smiles on their faces were priceless. They were beautiful, special children of God. I felt so at peace to know that I was able to give them something they would never have had. It was important to me for them to feel as much love as I could give them. Many had been neglected and their parents had abandoned them. At least I could show them my love. I wanted to do more, and tried with my entire being. I knew how it felt to feel unloved by a parent. Although these special children were severely disabled, they certainly had no disability when it came to feeling love.

Many of the children wore braces on their limbs. I had to do heavy lifting. They couldn't walk, so I lifted them from their chairs to wheelchairs or from their wheelchairs onto the toilet seat. I also lifted them from their wheelchairs onto the dining room chairs where they took their meals. As a result, I ended up with a hernia that required surgery. I had been at the school about one and half years then. I was upset that I would probably no longer be able to continue working with the children who I had grown to love. Sure enough, after my surgery, I was told that I could no longer do any heavy lifting, so I had to leave. This truly saddened me. I wanted to keep helping those children so badly. They were so severely handicapped that there was a limit to what one could do, which was quite frustrating.

With sadness, but also with inspiration, I left my position with a new goal: to obtain a degree in occupational therapy. For the first time in my life I had a thread of hope that maybe I could handle college. I did not want to pass up the opportunity to try. I did not want to be rejected again (as I had been when I attempted to enlist in the VISTA program) for not having received a degree in higher education. Having had the opportunity to experience this vocation was a wonderful experience, and it had proven to me beyond any doubt that my destiny was to help people less fortunate than me and help them believe in themselves.

In 1973 I applied as a volunteer in the Big Sister program with the Children's Protective Services in Salem. I loved working with kids and I felt I could make a difference in children's lives. I knew from past experiences that just knowing that someone cared could save a life. I knew firsthand. I could hang on to the thread of hope I had in my life knowing that my mom loved and needed me. I wanted to be able to do that for a child.

I was matched with an eleven-year-old girl named Molly. She was petite, blonde, and very shy. The first time we met was at her home in Salem. I was invited into her home where Molly's mom introduced us. I met her half-brother Ben and half-sister Jonnie. Ben and Jonnie were very outgoing and secure compared with Molly. It became clear to me that Molly felt unloved by her mom and very much alone. She felt like she was in the way in her home. Her mom had remarried and had Ben and Jonnie with her new husband. Molly felt like an outcast. This was reflected in her behavior. She did not get along with her peers and had no friends. She felt alone in a big world that didn't understand her. She did not do well in school and she didn't care. As I got to know Molly, I realized that her self-esteem was pretty low. She was in need of a special friend. I hoped that I would be able to add some joy to her joyless world.

I usually took her out on weekends. We went bowling, out to eat, shopping, and we managed to get our pictures in the newspaper doing something that kids usually only dream about—flying in the cockpit of a plane with a real pilot! The Aviation Science program at North Shore Community College where I had started to work sponsored a day for the Big Sister program. We got matched with a pilot who flew Molly and me over the North Shore area. It was exciting to see our own homes from a bird's eye view. I remember how excited Molly was and couldn't wait to tell her mom. Maybe this would get her some attention. We had a terrific time, and I think it may have been one of the most memorable experiences that Molly ever had. She had a smile from ear to ear that warmed my heart.

Molly was such a sad little girl. She didn't seem to know how to have fun, and I doubted that she'd had very much of it. She felt so alone and was very apprehensive in allowing herself to get close to anyone. She was a child who was hard to reach. She never really trusted anyone, but she often did confide in me. I remember she wrote me a letter once. She could not say these words to me, but she so wanted to, and so wrote them instead. This is what she wrote:

Dear Jacqui:

Thank you for being my big sister because you are so nice to me and you by[sic] things for me and I think are so nice of you. I am happy that I have you and you are so happy to have me did you know that. And did you tell you office people that I am you my best sister. I wrote this in school.

P.S. Write back O.K.

Love Molly

When Molly got older and entered high school she decided that she did not want to continue with our relationship any longer. After our two years together, I think she might have been trying to establish her independence. I respected her wishes and expressed to her that I would always be there for her.

In the end, Molly and I still talked on the phone but the phone calls became less frequent and they eventually stopped. I felt at this point I had done all I could. Molly knew I was there for her if she needed me. She called me years later and we talked about getting together, but she never carried through with it. I had no way of contacting her because she had told me she had no permanent address, and I didn't press her when she didn't offer to tell me where she was staying. She said she wasn't doing much with her life. She had quit school and gotten married to an older man. She had since divorced and was living on the streets. I wanted to meet with her badly, but I could not force my way into her life. I wanted to help her and give her a thread of hope in her saddened heart but I could never get in touch with her after that. I never heard from her again. I felt very saddened by this.

I found out a few years later in the local paper that Molly had died of a drug overdose. She was only thirty-five years old. I cried. I only hoped in my heart that she'd had some happy times during her time on earth, and that she'd held on to those times when she and I were "sisters." I know she is at peace now, and I hang onto that.

In 1976, I was elected to be on the Board of Directors of the North Shore chapter of St. Jude Children's Research Hospital. I was thrilled. St. Jude was my favorite saint and I was dedicated to the task of helping to find a cure to beat leukemia since my brother had died of it as a thirteen-year-old. Our Board focused on fundraising for the hospital. We had monthly meetings in the home of our chapter president and each of us would bring thoughts, concerns, and ways to help raise money to find a cure for leukemia. We held yard sales, hockey games, fund drives, golf tournaments, and an annual dinner dance to raise funds. The dinner dance was our greatest success. All of us worked hard for this great cause.

One year the national convention was held in Boston. It was a weekend-long event. I remember attending the conference and meeting so many dedicated people. The highlight for me was actually meeting Marlo Thomas, the daughter of actor and founder of St. Jude's Hospital, Danny Thomas. I remember watching *That Girl* on television. It starred Marlo Thomas, and I admired her character in it. She played a single woman living on her own who had an adorable boyfriend. She was cute, witty, and had a charismatic personality. I wanted to be just like her. Of course, at the conference I got to meet the man himself, too—Danny Thomas!

Early in Danny Thomas's career, he had made a promise to St. Jude that he would build a hospital if the saint would help him with his career. St. Jude must have fulfilled his wish because Danny Thomas had a very successful career. He didn't forget his promise. Marlo was chairperson of the hospital, and she was the guest speaker at the convention. I couldn't believe that my dream had come true. She was a wonderful, lovely, and gracious person. She had always been my idol.

The North Shore chapter of St. Jude continued for many years and eventually disbanded due to life's interruptions. Each of us continued on our own individual crusade and stayed committed in some way to helping the children of this great hospital. It was a truly rewarding experience for me. I think it helped me to know that even though Johnny did not survive this devastating illness, he did not die in vain. I was doing what I could to help in Johnny's name. I let him live through me.

There was a reason why God put Marguerite and me into each other's lives. Marguerite needed a friend and someone who could understand and care for her. I needed and wanted to help someone less fortunate than I. Marguerite was diagnosed with multiple sclerosis when she was thirty-five years of age. She had lost many of her friends who didn't understand the disease. When I first met Marguerite she introduced herself as "Peggy." So, I first knew her by that name. It was in our Theories of Personality class in graduate school that our instructor touched Peggy in a special way. One day Peggy told me that the instructor loved the name Marguerite. This was Marguerite's given name anyway. This was actually the instructor's name, too. Peggy decided that she wanted to be called by her birth name. From then on she asked me if I would address her as Marguerite.

Marguerite was married, a mother of two, and owned her own home with her husband Chris. A seizure, one of the side effects of her disease, took away her ability to maintain her teaching job. Her multiple sclerosis continued to get worse. It robbed her of her organizational skills and it also affected her short-term memory. She could no longer remember simple tasks or students' names or at times recognize their faces. This was devastating to Marguerite because teaching had been her life. Her motor skills and vision were also greatly affected.

When I first met Marguerite she was still struggling to complete her master's degree. She was having much difficulty, but would not give up. She used a walker, but sometimes was able to use a cane. Something compelled me to sit next to her in class. We got to be really good friends, and I became her advocate. She took "The Ride" (a shuttle service) to school, but shortly after I met her I volunteered to pick her up at her home and drive her back and forth to school. After class we usually went to Friendly's Restaurant for supper before returning home. There was never a time when we could sit down and eat a meal when someone didn't know Marguerite from her life as a teacher. Many of her students and parents recognized her. They all said what a wonderful teacher she was. After knowing her for only a short time, I could well understand what an inspirational teacher she had been. Sometimes Marguerite would not remember the students who remembered her, but she tried awfully hard.

I remember the day that Marguerite told me she felt it was time to give up her driver's license. I can't even imagine what a difficult decision it must have been for her. I drove her to the registry and we waited in a long line for assistance. We finally got to the counter and explained why we were there. Not one word came from that person's mouth. She just took the license and said, "Next." *Thanks a lot for your compassion,* I thought in my head. To the clerk it was just another piece of paper, but with it Marguerite was surrendering her independence. I am glad I was there to help her through her experience. This was only the beginning of the long chain of events that would occur.

Marguerite and I shared many experiences, all of which brought us close together as friends. I respected and admired her for the great courage she possessed. One time Marguerite and I went out to dinner after class. It was right after a snowstorm. As I tried to help Marguerite into my car she slipped and ended up half under the car on her back in the snow. I tried to help her up but she could not help herself and she was too much for me. She wasn't heavy, but she was "dead weight" and was in an awkward position. Her walker was in the middle of the parking lot. We were really quite a scene! Many people looked at us, but passed us by. All of a sudden this angel of a man came to our assistance and asked us if we needed help. We did—we admitted it. He helped Marguerite to her feet and then into my car and I was able to drive her safely home.

Marguerite suffered another massive seizure about a year after we met and was then confined to a wheelchair. She also had to leave the home she had loved so much. She had to reside in a nursing home instead. I visited her twice a week and took her out. The first nursing home Marguerite resided in was not a nice place, and eventually she moved to a residence closer to where her family and friends lived. This was tough for Marguerite. She had few friends left as many people who she'd once considered friends chose to avoid her. Marguerite spoke with slurred speech, which is often an effect of multiple sclerosis, and she was difficult to understand. She accepted the challenge with grace and dignity. We grew closer and I continued to be her friend and advocate. She always believed she would one day walk again. I believe this is what gave her the will to not give up. She never gave up hope.

A dear friend and colleague helped me organize a fundraiser for Marguerite. My friend, Kathy, is indeed an angel. She did not even know Marguerite, and yet donated her time, energy, and talents. She arranged for us to have this fundraiser at her church. We had a soup supper, for which volunteers made different kinds of soups and desserts. A local grocery store donated breads and rolls. We had coffee and tea. Tickets went for ten dollars and people who attended could have as much soup as they wanted. They got to keep the coffee mug that they chose. We had at least twenty different kinds of soup. We ended up making almost two thousand dollars. Other "angels" donated money toward Marguerite's fund just because they cared enough to do so. It was a wonderful event.

My friend, Kerry asked the parishioners to donate to our friend, Marquerite's fund at their church in Swampscott. It too was very successful and brought in a large amount of money. She was also a dear friend of Marguerite and had known her for years from living in the same neighborhood. They were also running buddies. Together we were on a mission to provide Marguerite with as comfortable lifestyle that we could give her. She deserved to have some comforts in life. Life had dealt her a bad deck. We bought Marguerite a remote recliner that she could maneuver by pressing a button. We also bought a beautiful television set and stand. One of Marguerite's principle enjoyments was watching sports on television. This was a perfect gift for her. She was able to see more clearly with the high definition set. We put the remainder of the money in a fund for her use. She used it to have her hair done or her nails nicely polished. We bought her clothes that she needed and any other incidental that she asked for. Marguerite believed her suffering was not in vain. Her tenacity was her "vessel," and she refused to ever give up the "oars." Marguerite passed away on December 8, 2006; the day of the Feast of the Immaculate Conception. I believe she sat on the angels' wings as they carried her into heaven.

I've always wanted others to know that there is a rainbow, no matter how black the sky can get. There is always hope even if it is only a thread. Life starts from a tiny seed, so hanging on to a thread of hope can open up the endless limits of the sky and create a beautiful rainbow.

There are many less fortunate people in the world who happen to fall on bad luck, some through no fault of their own and some otherwise. Regardless of the reason, everyone deserves a second chance and deserves to be respected and treated with dignity. My friend Terri was volunteering at a homeless shelter in Salem. After inquiring about what she did I became very interested in volunteering, too. She told me I could join her team. Our team provided breakfast to the homeless. Approximately every six weeks we bought the food and cooked a full meal. Breakfast usually consisted of eggs, bacon or sausage, toast and sometimes home fries, orange juice and coffee. There were times when we did not have enough food to go around and all we could provide them with was toast. Most were still grateful. In any event we were able to help those in need. My wish was that some day these less fortunate would have hope again. It didn't matter why they were there; what mattered was that each person was special and a child of God. I often wondered what the lives were like for the people who passed through the line for food. We might have been helping a doctor, for all we knew.

In August 2006, I organized a fundraiser for my goal group friend Terri's mom, Dorothy, who was in desperate need of an intestinal transplant. It had been a very long road for Dorothy, her family, and especially her dedicated, devoted daughter Terri. After much searching, wrong matches, and continuous infections our prayers were answered; a match was found. She received the transplant and takes one day at a time on her road to recovery.

I have always felt the need to help others. I have always been thankful for my blessings. I don't understand the ways of the world with all its unfairness and cruelty. The cruelty I have experienced has made me aware of how a little kindness can spark a light in someone's life. I know that I can make a difference just by caring and helping out any way I am able. As long as I am able to care, love, and assist individuals less fortunate, then I will continue to do so.

22

Family Matters

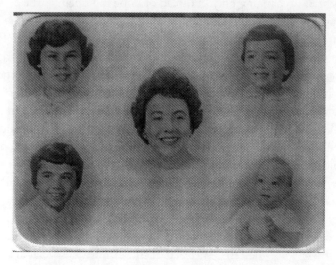

My Family-Jeanne, Debbie, Mom, Jacqui + Johnny

My family has always been a very important part of my life. There were many times when all we had were each other. The warmth, tenderness, and compassion that held us together gave us strength for the tears that came along in our lives. We bonded together, and together we survived the harsh realities of life. This is why it was so important to me to write this chapter of the book.

My sisters and I chose very different paths to follow. Although we grew up in the same house, we didn't live each other's lives. We all had our own personalities and our own unique way of surviving our childhood. It is amazing, as I look back, how very different I felt we were from one another. As we grew older, our viewpoints about life veered in independent directions. Our life choices were scarred by commonly afflicted, deep, ingrained injuries. We chose diverse ways to bandage our wounds, but the deep cuts that lay beneath kept us together in profound loss.

My sister Jeanne and I were very close growing up. We supported each other and helped each other through the tough years of our childhood. As the years passed by, we changed. Jeanne did not feel the way I did about our parents' situation, regarding in particular my father's relationship with the woman who became his other wife. She chose to have a relationship with my father's other wife so her children could have a relationship with their grandfather. I didn't understand at the time why she had made such a decision. My heart would not allow me to have any kind of relationship with his wife. I still was pained by not having a daddy who I felt loved me.

Jeanne moved to New Jersey and we no longer saw each other as often we would have liked. However, I loved my sister. I missed our closeness and missed seeing her. Though she married, moved on, and had children, we still retained our deep sense of love for each other. Our own personal theories and how each of us felt about life in general buried our feelings but never our love for each other.

She moved back to Massachusetts when her husband John got out of the service in 1972. Life went on and it was so wonderful to have her back, but with her busy life and mine it was very difficult to be in touch enough to share our feelings. We decided that we really needed to make it a point to regularly go out for dinner and just chat. The first time we went to a nice restaurant near where we both lived. We sat for hours and poured our hearts out to each other. We talked about long ago, and how very much we loved each other, and how we helped each other survive those terrible childhood days so long ago. We decided we had to continue to get together as often as we could.

I love Jeanne so much. Sometimes tragedies become a blessing in disguise. I believe this was the case for Jeanne and me. We had all suffered enough, and nothing could ever change what happened. Life goes on, though, and looking back just stops one from going forward.

Jeanne's husband John is an absolute peach. My sister was very fortunate to find such a caring and loving guy. John is genuine, and he and Jeanne are a perfect match for each other. He is extremely bright and has a great sense of humor. He has provided his family with a very comfortable life. He loves his wife and his children and has always shown them love through hard work, discipline, and empathy. He is truly unique. We get along great and he is always willing to help if he can. I consider myself very fortunate to have such a great brother-in-law.

My sister Debbie is five years younger than me. We have always had a close relationship. Debbie moved into my bedroom after Jeanne got married. She had

had to share a room with my brother Johnny before this. It was fun sharing a room with her. She was very neat and she was always cleaning our room. I remember I used to pay her to clean my share of it. She would not only dust but she would also polish all the furniture. She even vacuumed. She loved hanging curtains. I gladly paid her for a job I hated to do. My mom always said I should have been born rich, but since I wasn't I should spend the little money I had wisely.

Debbie and I had long talks. She confided in me about boyfriend issues and other concerns. Although Debbie was five years younger than me, she had a boyfriend before I had one. At the time we wore the same size clothes. I have to say, in this situation, I was the giver. She loved borrowing my clothes. I didn't mind, except that when I looked in our closet for a particular item to wear, more often than not it was missing. I didn't like the fact that I had to choose another outfit for the day. I started to choose my outfit for the next day the night before. If it was out of the closet, it was off limits to her. This seemed to work; well, most of the time.

She didn't have much of a relationship with my dad. He had left our home when she was seven, and before then he was hardly ever home anyway. She does remember my parents' horrific arguments. All of us do. Even as I write this, I can still hear the screams of each of their voices.

Debbie and I grew closer as she grew older. She, so to speak, caught up to me. She has always been a caretaker, too, always wanting to help others. She is divorced now, and I know that the echoes of her childhood constantly ring in her head. Her pain is deep, and she often confides in me about it. She considers me her friend, her counselor, and as I am always there for her, she is always there for me.

I love all my nieces and nephews. There are five in all. Jeanne and John have two children. Christine is the older one. She graduated from North Shore Community College and then from Syracuse University. She has always been very bright and has always excelled in everything she attempts. I remember one day I took her to work, thinking that it would be fun for her to see what I did during the day. She picked up a book that she saw lying on a table in my office and began reading. This was a college-level book. She was three years old. Once, a former boyfriend and I took Christine to the Edaville Railroad Park for the day. We took her on a train ride that we thought she would enjoy. As she stepped off the train, she became physically ill. She looked up at me with an expression that I will never forget. She said, "Auntie Jacqui, you know trains make me spit up!" My boyfriend and I looked at each other and couldn't help but laugh. Apparently she was smart enough to know that she didn't like train rides, and so surely thought I was smart enough to have known this, too.

Christine was an absolute cutie. One other time, when I was visiting her family, I held her in my arms and asked her how she was. She said, "Fine, Auntie Jacqui." My family then asked me how I was feeling, as this was while I was receiving chemotherapy, and I responded that I was doing okay. Christine must have picked up a negative vibe, though, because she looked at me with a solemn face and said, "Don't worry, Auntie Jacqui, everything will be alright," and then, with a slight pause, she said, "That's what I keep telling myself." This was hilarious coming out of a little girl's mouth, and so endearing. It made me laugh. I remember dreaming that I wanted a little girl just like her. She is married now, and has a great job as an editor. She lives in the western part of Massachusetts.

Michael, Christine's husband, is a lawyer. He is a kind and gentle man. He is also very bright. He can be quiet, but it is extremely interesting to converse with him on particular topics. His mom and dad, too, are friendly and thoughtful. We are lucky to have them as part of the family.

Christine's brother, my nephew John, is a fine young man. He has always been a teddy bear. His charm and wit have been his ticket out of many things and he knows how to use them to his full advantage. He is close to his mom and can do no wrong in her eyes. He is a very kind individual with a warmth about him that would melt butter in the depths of an Alaskan winter. He was always very active as a child and kept Jeanne busy. She was constantly trying to find ways to calm him. We often joked about hiding him in a drawer because he was like a jack-in-the-box. He just wouldn't wind down.

When John was about four years old; my sister threw a birthday party for him. She wanted to have a clown at his party so I volunteered. I borrowed a clown outfit, which covered me from head to ankle, but I didn't have clown shoes. I borrowed my sister's furry slippers and went outside and rang the doorbell. I remember hearing someone telling John to answer the door. He came to the door and opened it wide. The expression on his face was hilarious. He had a smile wider than the Grand Canyon. I asked him if I could come in and he nodded for me to enter. As Johnny looked the "clown" up and down, his smile disappeared, and he said, "Look, everybody, this clown has my mommy's slippers on!" I began to laugh, but my little nephew was not happy with his clown who'd somehow gotten his mother's slippers. He made me take the slippers off and give them back to his mom. This was something I will never forget. John went on to become an Eagle Scout and eventually graduated from high school and college. He has a job in management, married a wonderful woman named Sarah, and lives with her in Massachusetts.

Sarah graduated from Suffolk University with high honors. She is quite bright. Her love of politics landed her a job in the State House. She met my nephew while he was a chaperone at a party Debbie threw for her daughter, and Sarah was a guest. She makes my nephew very happy, and they are very much in love. They have their own home and love it.

My sister Debbie has three children. My niece, Meaghan Elizabeth, is a beautiful young woman. Even as a child she was a perfectionist. If she received a ninety percent for a grade it upset her. She never felt she was "perfect" enough. She graduated from high school and excelled in everything. She wanted to learn the piano, and she did. She took Spanish and was able to master it in no time at all. She learned to dance. She was in a dance recital where she learned the steps to *Riverdance* flawlessly.

Meaghan went through some emotional trauma when her parents divorced. She suffered in the wake of their divorce. After high school, Meaghan decided she wanted to attend college. She started her freshman year at North Shore Community College but withdrew, deciding that school was not for her at that time in her life. She moved out of my sister's home for a while until she found out the hard way that she truly needed an education. She moved back home and reenrolled at North Shore Community College. She is now taking liberal arts for a major. She has high hopes for herself, and she has the ability to succeed. She has a lifetime ahead of her and I believe she will succeed in whatever she chooses to do. I believe in her, and I love her very much.

My niece Ashleigh is as kind and warm as her mom. She has always been the sweet and gentle one in the family. She is a beautiful young woman inside and out. We are very close and she is very loving toward everyone. She graduated from high school in 2005. She attends college and is majoring in psychology. She works part time and is her mom's "right arm." She has plenty of support behind her. She loves to write and read and she enjoys helping those around her. She went through the same ordeal as her sister with their parents' divorce, and has found it very difficult to understand the reasons behind their breakup. She was quiet, but likely carried some pain and the burden of trying to make everything better. She would learn that she had no control over what happened to her parents. She wasn't to blame, and she had to learn to live her own life. She reminds me of how I was as a child, trying to make it all right. She is a very deep person who has much to offer and a lifetime to achieve whatever she wants to do.

My nephew Brandon, Debbie's youngest, is adorable. He is currently in high school and is truly a charmer. He is extremely bright and loves school. He loves to learn and catches on quite quickly to any task given to him. He is mechanically inclined and can piece together any objects set before him. He can take a quick glance at directions, and, *poof,* the pile of materials transforms into a beautiful piece. Brandon is a sensitive child who adores his mom and tries to help her in any way he can. He also loves his dad and they have been able to keep up a relationship in which they spend time together on a weekly basis. Brandon often feels burdened with his loyalties to both of his parents. He loves his mom, but he also loves his dad. His dad remarried, which puts additional stress on Brandon in dealing with his feelings. I know he struggles with feeling okay about liking his dad's new wife, and wonders whether it is a betrayal to his mom. I feel for him and the pain he has suffered through this tough transition.

I love all of the members of my family—each and every one of them. We are all unique in our own way. We each have something to offer the world, and the world has something to offer us. No one is perfect and to strive to be perfect is fruitless. To be a good person and to do the best one can is all that should be expected. We have ourselves to answer to; for it is ourselves with whom we live. I do not judge any of my family members and only wish them the very best. It is because of my family and their support that I am living a wonderful life. Family has helped sustain me in all my struggles. When I felt hopeless, helpless, and alone, and not wanting even to live, my family was always in the back of my mind, helping me choose to make it. Today I realize how they are the strong roots of my survival and how they are what I hold onto today. They say you can pick your friends but not your relatives. Well, this is the family I would choose.

23

Traveling Around

I wanted to include this chapter in my book because travel has been a very positive part of my life. Traveling was also an escape route for me at one time. I felt like a bird when I was traveling: beyond anyone's reach, free and happy. It has always fascinated me that it is possible to take a plane ride and in a matter of hours be clear across the country, or on another continent.

Traveling has helped me grow as a person, and it has taught me to appreciate more of how lucky I truly am. It confirms for me what I was already aware of, that I live in a country that has so much to offer. It certainly is the land of the free. My travels throughout the U.S. have shown me that although the people of our beautiful country are not free from pain, sorrow, and many injustices, we certainly enjoy a land of opportunity and choice. I feel that we are the most fortunate nation in the entire world. I feel grateful that I was born in the U.S.A.

That said, we live in a big world and I wanted to see as much of it as I could. Traveling throughout the world is one of the great passions of my life. When I think about traveling a thrill passes through me. It has always given me a sense of excitement and control because I could choose where I wanted to go. I could visit places where nobody knew me. I felt carefree and I was able to relax. I was able to just be me.

I was able to travel with friends and family some of the time, too, who also enjoyed their time away from home. I never wanted my journeying to end, but when a trip was over I just set my sights on the next one.

The year that I graduated from high school I took my mom to New York City. I had saved my money the entire year so I would be able to treat her as my guest—all expenses paid. We flew there on Eastern Airlines. I remember paying twenty-one dollars for my mom's ticket and nineteen dollars for mine, round trip. Even back then this was a great price. We stayed near Forty-second Street at the Taft Hotel, a very nice accommodation with many amenities. We took a tour of NBC studios and were able to get tickets to the Merv Griffin Show where

Eartha Kitt was the special guest star. We attended a Rockettes performance at the renowned Radio City Music Hall. We strolled along the famous streets and shopped, and took a tour of the city, which included the infamous Bowery. We saw vendor after vendor cooking up their peppers and sausages that they sold at reasonable prices. The aroma alone persuaded any person passing by to at least consider indulging in one of its delicacies.

One evening my mom and I got brave and decided to see a midnight movie. As we walked through the brightly colored streets we saw make-believe nuns "collecting money for the poor." These con artists were dressed up in black habits and held rosary beads. They gave a convincing portrayal as sisters seeking funds to help the underprivileged. The police approached them and asked them to leave. They did. We passed beggars who worked the busy streets and alleyways, desperate for coins. Venturing out at midnight was something in and of itself; however, it was the movie that we chose that made our evening really exciting. The movie was *Rosemary's Baby*. It was really spooky and seemed so real. To this day I can still remember the line, when one of the warlocks says to Rosemary about her newborn baby, "Rosemary, he has his father's eyes!" There was no need to see the baby in the film because a vivid picture of that baby appeared in my mind. Rosemary's face held a look of horror that said it all. Afterward, we were anxious to get back to the hotel. I think I checked under the bed before retiring for the evening. What an experience!

I was so excited that my mom enjoyed our trip to New York. I was so glad to be able to make her happy and finally to get to try to make up for what she had missed and truly deserved. Although I couldn't take her to an exotic place, New York was a good beginning. It made my heart smile. I got a sense of worth being able to take my mom on a trip, too. I felt good, and continued my quest to please her and planned through the years many other trips, including a stay in San Diego, a vacation in sunny Florida, and the most memorable excursion of all: a trip to Paris, France, including a visit to Lourdes, located in the mountains.

But our next memorable trip was much more local. We went to Cape Cod, Massachusetts. My girlfriend Kathy had introduced me to Cape Cod when she had invited me to spend the weekend with her at her parents' summerhouse. Crossing the Sagamore Bridge had felt like traveling to another world. I had fallen in love with Cape Cod immediately. Kathy had given me a tour of many of the nice spots at the Cape and I had taken a lot of notes and gathered attraction brochures. I knew then that Cape Cod was one place I wanted to take my mom. I knew she would love it just like me. The trip was a perfect birthday gift to present to her on her birthday, May 30. That day she opened her card and read the inserted note. She was so excited. She had never been to Cape Cod.

We stayed at a place called the Soundings in Dennis, MA. Our motel was directly on the ocean and had indoor and outdoor swimming pools. The beach had beautiful white sand and the color of the water was glorious. We had a room with a breath-taking ocean view. At night we kept our windows ajar and listened to the calming sounds of the seagulls' cries and enjoyed the scent of the salt-water air. It was very peaceful. It was a place I didn't want to leave and surely wanted to visit again.

At the Cape we discovered a great shopping place called The Christmas Tree Shop. It had great bargains! We walked the beaches of the Cape, took a boat trip up to Provincetown, visited historic Hyannis, and enjoyed the warm sunshine that I felt was not the same sun I had left on the North Shore. I knew this would not be my last trip to the Cape. I found a little piece of paradise there.

I traveled to Nova Scotia, Canada, with my friend Nancy in August 1974. I had always wanted to go on a cruise, though I didn't know where, exactly; but I knew I wanted to experience the pleasure of it all. I had heard so much about how there was nothing like it and I wanted to find out for myself. We couldn't afford a major cruise company, but we were satisfied with plans for a short cruise with the Prince of Fundy cruise lines. Our ship was called the Bolero. We thought it was great. We were impressed with its swimming pool, large restaurant, coffee shop, gambling casino, elevators, and duty-free shop. It amazed us how all of these things could be on a relatively small craft sailing way out into the ocean. I remember our cabin was small but quite sufficient and it had its own bathroom—a must for us.

We traveled overnight and enjoyed our views of the ocean and feeling the sea breezes brush against our skin. In the morning we arrived in Yarmouth, Nova Scotia, and registered at the Grand Hotel where we would enjoy an overnight stay. We wanted to make the most out of our mini vacation. There wasn't a lot to do in Yarmouth and we didn't have enough time to venture out to the bigger city of Halifax so we visited a few local shops. The people we met were extremely nice. We had fun and returned on our ship back home on the following day.

Also in 1974, my girlfriend Louise and I went on a chartered tour to Mexico. The trip included airfare, hotel, transfer to and from the hotel, and land tours. Louise was my sister's sister-in-law. She was the same age as me and we had a lot in common. She was very close to her family and she had two sisters, too, so we could share sister stories with each other. We were both extremely close to our families, especially our mothers. We learned a lot about each other and shared many of our thoughts, joys, and fears. We had a lot of the same insecurities and it felt good to be able to share feelings with someone who would not be critical of me or judgmental. I could be open with her about the way I felt about life. I wanted to love life and I wanted to find the key to unlock the world I had lived in before the darker days of my childhood. She was warm and such a good listener. We are dear friends to this day.

Louise and I were both single and we had similar interests. One of our common interests was that we both loved to travel. We spent three days together in Mexico City. The city was huge—unlike any other city I had ever visited. It had many old buildings and was very historic. We climbed the great pyramids, visited unique shops, and took the opportunity to visit the American Embassy. We tasted the different foods at the unique and quaint restaurants and experienced the culture of the Mexican people. We got to know how to negotiate the currency (peso), learning its exchange rate quickly. Because we were on a tour we had little or no problem with a language barrier. The English-speaking tour guide took care of us quite well, and we didn't venture away too much on our own.

After a three-day stay in Mexico City, we traveled by bus to a silver mining town called Taxco. It had great little shops where you could get bargains of a lifetime if you knew how to bargain. Merchants sold leather pocket books that you could get for a fraction of the price you would pay in the States, and silver rings and jewelry for practically nothing, too. It definitely was a tourist stop because what we saw beyond the town limits would make one cry. This region of Mexico was very, very poor. The trip along the way to Taxco had been lined with small shacks. We could see that there was no indoor plumbing, and some shacks did not even have doors. I remember seeing chickens running wild and little, shoeless kids playing outside in tattered clothes. It was sad to see them stare at our passing bus, as if they hoped it would stop but it never did. Children sat on the edges of the dirt road with crooked legs. When they stood they were unable to walk upright, and begged for American coins. It broke my heart. Elderly women made handmade straw baskets to sell—holding them up to our windows as our bus passed by. I wanted to get off the bus, give them all a hug, and pass out some coins to each and every one of them, but the bus didn't stop.

The tour guide warned us not to give the children or the beggars any money. But giving money to these unfortunate souls had been my first thought. He then told us an unbelievable story about how parents broke the legs of their newborn babies so their legs would grow crooked. They would then send the children out to beg for money. The theory is that people always feel badly for unfortunate children, and their pity entices them to help them. It was hard to believe that parents would do such a terrible thing to a child especially their own child, but apparently they did. Many of the children were born with multiple handicaps regardless, due to lack of medical attention. It was a real eye opener for me, and so sad.

I remember thinking how lucky I was and how fortunate that I got to live in a beautiful, free country that offered endless opportunities. Our land, our country, our United States of America was a land full of opportunity and wealth. I felt blessed. How could I ever complain about anything? These people were lucky to share a cup of rice with their family members. Clean water? I don't even think they knew the possibility. I have to say I was glad when we left that area, although it never left my head or my heart. Our next stop was Acapulco.

Acapulco, Mexico, was absolutely beautiful. We knew we were at a luxurious resort as soon as we'd arrived. Beautiful flowers graced the entrance and the landscape was exquisite. Our hotel was directly on a beach with white sand. The ocean water was 88 degrees, and the air temperature was a balmy 105. This was quite a contrast from Mexico City where the temperature had been in the high seventies. It was totally different from what we had experienced on our trip through Taxco and the villages along the way. We enjoyed our stay, but my thoughts often drifted back to the poor people that we had seen en route. We took walks on the beach, ate good food, took in some evening entertainment and, of course, shopped. We flew back to Mexico City for our last night before we went home. I will never forget this trip for all it taught me.

In May 1975 I traveled alone to visit my friend in beautiful San Diego, California. I was visiting my girlfriend Barbara who was living there at the time. Her boyfriend was stationed at the navy base in San Diego, and she had invited me out to visit her. One of my dreams had been to go to California and visit Disneyland and this was my chance. I was excited about my new adventure. I arrived on May 17 at 8:15 AM. Our first stop was McDonalds. All that way, and my first stop was McDonalds! Oh well. I was in for a treat. My girlfriend was happy to have a visitor from back home, and she was the most gracious hostess. We didn't stop doing incredible things the entire time I was there.

The first full day I was there we went to Mass at this very beautiful church. Of course I made my three wishes. I knew I had never been in that church before so I wished away. I am sure I wished for health, and I probably wished that God would guide me and help me find someone in my life, and the third was probably for my family. We ate breakfast and visited Sea World. I remember the day was hot, and as we sat on the bleachers and watched the dolphins and seals. I thought about how nice it would be to join them in the clear, cool pool of water where they entertained us. Of course I didn't join them, but I was tempted. That afternoon we went to see the Ice Follies. What a contrast. I hadn't seen the Ice Follies since I was a child. That evening we dined at a fancy restaurant. This was a beautiful end to a glorious day.

The next day was just as exciting. We got up early and visited the Old Town candle shop. We visited Del Mar with the beautiful condominiums that had ocean views of Point Loma. We shopped at La Jolla and ended the day with a visit to Laserium, a space theater. On Tuesday, we went shopping in Coronado and visited the San Diego Zoo. In the evening we dined at a dinner show at the Ramada Inn where we were entertained by a belly dancer. Wednesday proved to be most intriguing. We took a drive to the Yuma Desert in Arizona. It was only after we played in the sand like children did we realize that there might have been scorpions underneath us. I shiver even now with the thoughts of what could have happened. It was a very exciting day, but Thursday was unforgettable. We traveled to Tijuana, Mexico. As we entered over the border many children approached us begging for coins. It broke my heart all over again. Many of the children were crippled, shoeless, wore tattered clothes, and used a stick to help them walk. I asked myself how could anyone live like this. I thanked God for blessing me. On Friday we dined at the Del Coronado hotel. We then drove to Los Angeles and toured the big city. We ended our day on the beautiful ship Queen Mary where we dined before leaving for home.

Time was going by too fast. I wanted this trip to last forever. It was already Saturday and we had so much more to see and do. We got up early and drove to Beverly Hills. There we went on a tour of the homes of Art Linkletter, Dean Martin, and David Jansen, to name a few. Although we could not enter their homes, we got beautiful views of the outside. Our visit included Grauman's Chinese Theatre, where we saw the hand and footprints of many stars, including Shirley Temple, Lucille Ball, and John Wayne, among others. We went to a wax museum where you would bet your life the figures were real. We went to my long-awaited Disneyland, and spent another full day of fun and adventure. Sunday was my last day and I wasn't going to waste a single minute of it. We toured Universal Studios. It was fascinating to discover how the stunts were performed, how the Red Sea was parted on a set, how fire and other dangerous phenomenon are made to look so real. It was amazing to see. I would forever remember this experience.

My next big adventure was to travel to the beautiful state of Hawaii. My friend Marie was going to join me, and we were ready to experience a joy of a lifetime. We were really looking forward to this trip. It was February and the dead of winter. It was cold, snowy, and icy, and this wintry month was a month we wanted to leave behind us in New England. Nothing sounded better to us than a trip to the islands of Hawaii. The thoughts of the tropical sun were heavenly. Unfortunately for Marie, she was unable to fulfill her dream because her car was stolen, which caused her a lot of worry and the need to save her money. As for me, I decided that I would go even if I had to go alone. At the time, I was taking classes at North Shore Community College. One day, I shared my story of woe to a woman in my class. She listened, and after a moment she said, "I'll go with you." I couldn't believe it. I didn't know this woman very well, but she seemed nice enough. Her name was Carol. She called the travel agency to transfer Marie's reservations to her name. We spoke with each other on the phone, and after class, and got to know each other better. I had a good feeling that traveling with Carol was going to work out just fine.

For $399.00, all-inclusive, we flew to Hawaii on a 747 jet that had a spiral staircase that led up to a full service bar, but I felt high enough so I didn't indulge. We arrived at the airport and were greeted by a beautiful Hawaiian woman who put freshly cut leis of flowers around our necks and gave us a little peck on the cheek. She greeted us warmly to Hawaii.

The island was glorious and abundantly sunny. It was also peaceful, serene, and carefree. We stayed at the luxurious Outrigger, directly on the beach. We went on numerous land tours that included the Polynesian Cultural Center, a tour of the Dole pineapple manufacturing site, and a visit to an area called the North Shore. This area was a big attraction for tourists who were into surfing. We also attended a luau that was held right on our beach. We also visited Pearl Harbor, which left us reflecting on how horrible it must have been for all those people and how it had certainly left an indelible mark on history. I still can vividly remember Pearl Harbor today.

The Polynesian Cultural Center might have been my favorite tour. A little trolley drove us around and stopped at the different sites. We could get on and off at any site that drew our interest. We visited a hut where the women taught us how to weave baskets and the men taught us about silver mining. We took a lesson in hula dancing, which was a real hoot. It was a most memorable day.

Night entertainment was not lacking, from sword throwers to dancing there was plenty to see and do. There were also many dinner shows to choose from at various prices. It was at one of these dinner shows where I tried a fish called Mahi-Mahi. It was described as a white fish so I didn't think I had anything to lose. It wasn't until years later that I found out that mahi-mahi is *dolphin*! Then, all I could think of was, *I ate Flipper! Flipper* was a television show in the sixties. I remember later when I traveled to Florida and was dining in a restaurant I came across mahi-mahi. In small print, I read on the menu, "Not Flipper." I was happy about that although I wondered if he had already been eaten. I asked the waitress if a lot of people asked her if they would be eating Flipper, and so they'd had to print the disclaimer, and she told me that, indeed, that's why the sign was in the menu. She cleared up the confusion telling me that mahi-mahi is a dolphin fish, but not technically dolphin. I am glad she set me straight. Anyway, my Hawaiian vacation proved to be one of my best.

I love the United States of America. We have a beautiful country. Every state has its own unique beauty, Hawaii certainly being one of them. Matt and I fulfilled a dream of ours when we traveled across the country in the summer of 1978. We started from Massachusetts, and oh, what a trip it was. It would take many pages if I went into detail about all we did and all we saw. So I will share in some of the highlights that I most remember and in the order that I enjoyed most.

We swam in the Great Salt Lake in Utah and floated on top of the water. We visited the Grand Canyon, and the amazing Hoover Dam in Arizona. We stopped to see the corn fields of Nebraska, stood in a place called the Four Corners Monument, where you could actually be in four states at the same time: Arizona, New Mexico, Utah, and Colorado. This was a very popular tourist stop.

On our return, we stopped at a place called "South of the Border" on the border of North and South Carolina. This American landmark had been advertised all along the long stretch of highway with signs that read, "Pedro says, 400 miles to South of the Border," "Pedro Says, 350 miles to South of the Border," and so on, and so on. The excitement built, as I wanted to see this place that these giant billboards made seem so intriguing. It ended up just being a gigantic tourist trap filled with gifts shops. Key chains, little Pedro mugs, banners, cigarette lighters—you name it, and Pedro had it.

We spent a day at the Grand Ole Opry in Tennessee where we saw many talented hopefuls and enjoyed a terrific show in the Opryland Theater. The Opryland Park was filled with amusement rides, games, and entertainment. We continued our journey up to Hershey Park in Pennsylvania where the streetlights are shaped like Hershey Kiss candies. It was another amusement park but unique in its own right.

The visit to an Amish farm was interesting, as was all of the Pennsylvania Dutch country. We were allowed into one of the Amish homes to see how plainly they lived. The living room was set up so that their exquisite quilts and handcrafted items were beautifully displayed for purchase. The home was designed in very basic décor. Gas lanterns lit the house. The furniture was simple and unadorned. We were able to meet some Amish children who were courteous but not overly friendly. The Amish seemed trustworthy. I found that the woman who was selling her quilts took Master Charge or Visa, which interested me, but used a hand-operated processor for transacting the cards.

We also visited Busch Gardens in Virginia. We had a nice stopover in Maryland where we visited friends and enjoyed the famous Maryland crab legs. We visited Washington D.C., which I found very congested. We wanted to visit the White House but as luck would have it the White House was closed on Mondays, which was the day we were there. It was crowded with cars, buses, taxi, and many, many people going about their business. The city had a certain coldness about it. Near to D.C. we visited the Arlington National Cemetery, the resting place of our beloved president, John F. Kennedy.

Our final stop was New York before heading home. Needless to say, we enjoyed our entire cross-country trip. We gained so much knowledge about our beautiful country as we traveled across it. It was an education in itself and a fun way to learn. It gave me peace and a true sense of freedom. It was a fabulous trip and Matt and I had a great time together. I couldn't believe that I had actually lived one of my dreams.

In 1979, I visited my pen pal Prisca, who was from Costa Rica, Central America. I met her through my friend Ali. Ali lived in the U.S. and worked at the college with me. Prisca was Ali's sister, and I met her when she was visiting Ali in the U.S. Ali and Prisca's parents were missionaries at one time in Costa Rica. They had brought up their family there.

I enjoyed learning about Costa Rican culture. I visited during the month of December, just before the Christmas holiday. When I arrived, the temperature was in the high seventies. It was absolutely beautiful there and just my kind of winter day. Since I am a person who thrives in warm to hot weather this was perfect for me. I stayed at Prisca's apartment in the city of San Jose. She lived next to her mom and siblings. Everyone was so cordial. Naturally, they were fluent in Spanish but they were also fluent in English. Actually, my friends' family had dual citizenship: they were all American and Costa Rican citizens. My friend Ali was visiting then, too. Her presence made my stay in Costa Rica even more comfortable for me.

San Jose was beautiful, but I remember feeling a little touch of home when I saw a Sears store in the city, and a MacDonald's. I remember seeing little children pressing their noses up against the front windows of the restaurant, most likely dreaming of being able to go into the restaurant to order a burger and fries. It was sad to see and will forever be embedded in my mind. As I glanced at all the businesses along one typical street in San Jose that ranged from banks, to federal offices, private companies, and retail stores, I noticed that only one building had air conditioning units in several of its windows. The windows of the other buildings were open or stuffed with fans. I asked my friend what company or agency was fortunate enough to afford the air conditioners. Her reply: The American Embassy. What could I say?

My friend wanted me to see all of Costa Rica, especially the Pacific Ocean side. We traveled to a well-known tourist spot: a gorgeous beach called Jaco Beach. This was the highlight for me. The hotel was delightful and was directly on the beach. The temperature was in the nineties, quite a contrast from the mountainous region of San Jose, which had been in the 70-degree range. We had a wonderful time at Jaco beach. We dined at an outdoor café where I enjoyed the warmth of the sun on my face. The people were extremely nice. I remember them asking me if I spoke Spanish. They graciously spoke English to me when I replied negatively, and I doubled my efforts to learn as much as I could in the very short time I was there. Costa Rica was an incredible adventure, and not one I'll soon forget.

It was May 23, 1983 when my mom and I took off for the Bahamas. We stayed at the Harbour Cove Hotel, directly over the ocean. What a trip it was. The weather was no less than perfect and the people were so nice. I remember beautiful, white sand beaches and crystal clear water that was a temperature to die for. Our resort had two beautiful pools. One of the pools was a swim-up bar pool where you could sit on a stool in the water and order a nice cooling tropical drink. The part of the island where our hotel and resort was located was breath taking. Beautiful buildings were graced with sweet-smelling tropical flowers and the streets were sparkling clean. I could understand why this region of the Bahamas was called Paradise Island.

The contrast that we later saw broke our hearts. We walked over the long bridge that connected Paradise Island to the island capital of Nassau. The area right off of the island bridge was very, very poor. The houses were shacks. People on the streets begged. We found a Dunkin Donuts there, however, which felt like a touch of home. Despite the obvious poverty surrounding us, I knew that real estate there was extremely expensive, and I wondered how the people who lived there could afford to buy donuts when they probably couldn't even afford to buy milk for their children. It came to mind that it was probably tourists like us who ventured over the bridge that kept them afloat. Our departure back to the States was on May 30, my mom's birthday. We'd had a wonderful trip and a memorable experience.

I vacationed in Aruba in April 1985. My mom and I needed to get away, and we'd heard so many good things about Aruba that we wanted to find out for ourselves if these things were true. The people on the island of Aruba were by far the friendliest people we had ever met. They were genuine and helpful. The weather was absolutely beautiful! The temperature of the island hovered around 85 degrees the entire time we were there. We were fortunate that we were not there during the hurricane season, however. The water was luscious and the beaches beyond gorgeous. We stayed at a small, two-story hotel called the Manchebo. It had the only nude beach on the island. Although I didn't skinny dip, we did get to see one "bathing beauty." We noticed that there was a man with binoculars sitting at the bar looking onto the beach. He was completely oblivious to any other thing going on. It was more entertaining to watch him than what was going on at the beach.

The food was delicious, but expensive. Luckily, we had the food plan in our vacation package so we were able to dine on their famous giant crab legs. *Yum, Yum.* We tried many of the island dishes and enjoyed experiencing some new ones. We visited the downtown area and all the unique shops. Across the street from our hotel was a casino. We aren't big gamblers, but one couldn't help but be filled with the excitement of the clanking of the coins. We loved seeing the bright lights and hearing the sounds of bells ringing as someone hit it big. We had fun playing the slots, but kept to our commitment and allowed ourselves only so much to lose. The entire trip was fabulous, and is one of our most memorable trips.

September 1989 was the first time I traveled to Europe. This was to honor the aforementioned promise I'd made to the Blessed Mother of God that if she helped me through my cancer ordeal, I would make a pilgrimage to Lourdes in thanksgiving. I knew it was a huge promise and a big expense, but that I would find a way to fulfill it because it was important to me to do so. I went to a travel agency to make arrangements and I found an inclusive land and airfare deal. It included round trip flight to Paris and transfers to and from a hotel, for five days and four nights. This sounded like a great base, but I still needed to find my way to Lourdes. The travel agent was most accommodating and arranged for a secondary plane ride to Lourdes, including two overnight stays at a local hotel in the area.

Paris was absolutely stunning. It had great architecture and wonderful little shops. We visited the Louvre and saw the Mona Lisa. We ate at many of the outdoor cafés and enjoyed the beauty of the city and its culture. The people of Paris walked the streets; many holding water bottles, and often some Parisians carried a baguette of French bread. This was a common sight in Paris but personal water bottles were not yet being enjoyed in the States. Today many Americans walk around with their "specialty" water, minus the bread.

Lourdes ended up being four hundred miles from Paris. It was very mountainous and very cold and rainy while my mom and I were there. However, I didn't really care about how cold or uncomfortable it was. Finally, I had fulfilled my promise. I was actually at Lourdes. I was very disappointed with what I saw outside the gates of Lourdes, though. It was so commercialized. There were hundreds of vendors selling all kinds of religious articles, and despite their dubious quality they weren't cheap. This bothered me a lot. It was truly a moneymaking market.

However, inside the gates was a beautiful basilica. Many pilgrims were there, hoping and praying for a miracle. Wheelchairs, crutches, and canes leaned up against the walls of the basilica, left behind by the "cured." Holy music filled the space with *Ave Maria* and other hymns. People prayed on their knees and crawled to the large altar that held statues of Mother Mary, St. Joseph, Our Lord Jesus, and many others.

I have had a strong devotion to Our Lady of Lourdes ever since I was a young child and I had first learned about St. Bernadette. I always admired Bernadette and thought about how special she was to have actually seen Mary. She was given many gifts. I had always been taught that Jesus never says no to his mother. I felt that my prayers there would be answered. I had always prayed, but being in Lourdes somehow made me feel my prayers were louder and could be more clearly heard. This is probably not true, but I felt since I had made the extra effort to travel across the ocean and many miles from home that maybe it counted more. I know some people might say, "Why not go right to the top?" meaning, directly to God, but I say "a little intercession" never hurt. Anyway, it worked for me. I said my novenas, made my requests, and said my prayers. I am still alive and well. I had fulfilled my promise and my dream. *Amen.*

Las Vegas is the city of lights. This place is alive and never takes a nap. On a whim, my friend Lynne and I decided we wanted to go on a vacation. We had to find a place that both of us would enjoy, didn't cost a lot, and wasn't too far from home. However, we wanted to fly. She found a great deal that was less than four hundred dollars including hotel, airfare, and transfers. We arrived at the Circus, Circus Hotel in Las Vegas. It wasn't fancy, but we loved it. It was clean, had its own casino, nice restaurants and shops, and of course, great circus acts. We gambled a little, saw a great show, and stayed out until we were exhausted. We walked the Strip and stopped in many of the hotels, which put us in awe. The beautiful colors, gorgeous flowers, palm trees, and the many different people that we encountered added to the excitement of our fabulous getaway. We came back with great memories.

Marco Island, Florida, deserves a section of it own. It is a spectacular place. It has a beauty of its own. It is located south of Naples, Florida, on the west coast, and promises not to disappoint its visitors. The beaches and the water are incredible. It is directly on the Gulf of Mexico. Water temperatures in June through October range between 84 and 88 degrees—not too shabby. The island is small, and easy to get to by land, air, or sea. It is getting well known now and I fear someday it will be too crowed to visit. There was a theater where its patrons can dine while they watch the show. The island is filled with unique shops. Cruises to the Keys make an interesting day trip and snorkeling is a great activity. A trolley ride is a great way to see the island. Manatees swim so close to shore that people can actually touch them. Marco Island is definitely a little piece of paradise.

Prince Edward Island was absolutely amazing. I had always wanted to visit that province of Canada. We went on a bus tour that proved to be an excellent way to see it. The island offers much to do with a tranquility that can be compared to none. We traveled over the seventeen-mile bridge across the river, which was amazing and a sight to see. The little shops in quaint towns each had a story of their own and made our travel to the island even more pleasant. The reverse hill where cars climb backward up the hill leaves one in awe: *How can that be?* This beautiful little island has the freshest and cleanest air; this is just an added feature to a place that is hard to beat.

Life is too short to waste a minute. I am not rich, but I am very wealthy. I am able to work and save money to be able to travel, and I am healthy enough to have the energy and strength to endure the fatigue one can have by traveling. I am not afraid to venture out and explore the beautiful world we have. Traveling started out by being an escape for me. It was a way I could be somewhere where no one would know me. Now, traveling is my favorite pastime.

The many people I have met along the way and the interesting places I have visited have enriched my life and helped me grow as a person. At times my journeys made me laugh, they made me cry, and they made me humble, but most of all they helped me appreciate life for everything it has to offer.

24

Reflections

I look at life as a journey; a road that has many twists and turns. Parts of the road I have traveled were comforting, nurturing, and rewarding. Other parts of the road were dangerous, sorrowful, and full of struggles and trauma. In my life, I have always been searching to find out who I was. Some times in my life have been quite painful, but I always managed to hang on to a thread of hope when I felt almost completely hopeless. My search has been long. I sometimes wanted to die but something kept me hanging on to the hope that maybe, just maybe, I would find my way to being happy.

I feel blessed. Many times over, my faith has guided me through tough times; not any particular religion but my faith. I believe in Jesus Christ, and believe that when I pray to Him, He hears my every word. He has guided me and has given me strength. I believe that He is stronger than any evil that exists. I often hear people wonder, "Why would God do this?" I don't believe that God sends us "bad" things. He is all-good. It is the evil of the world that doles out the malevolence in the world. I simply believe that the times when I'm being challenged the most are when I need God the most. If I didn't feel there was justice in the end, I don't know how I would handle my life. I know that with God, justice prevails.

Life has a lot to offer. I now focus on what I have in my life versus the things that I still find myself sometimes desiring. My philosophy in life has changed over the years. I look at my life through its seasons. Each season of my life has been as drastically different as the New England seasons passing through each and every year. Do I like the dark season of the ruthless winter cold that has visited my life? No, however, it has helped me grow and has given me a greater appreciation for life and all of its beauty. Hopefully, each experience makes the next lesson in life easier, and I will continue to grow even more from those to come.

Happiness is found within. I realized that after spending a lot of time looking outside myself for happiness. Not finding it, I became disappointed, helpless, and felt like I had no control over my life. If someone or something didn't work out the way I had hoped, I usually became depressed. It is only when I learned to look inside my own heart and soul that I found that I had the control all along to allow happiness into my life. I cannot always control what might happen, but I can control how I am going to handle and feel about the situation. Life has great meaning and it has many doors. Sometimes I open the wrong door, but I learn from the experience and that is what has made my suffering not in vain. I have grown stronger because of it. I believe we all go through life only once, so why not make the best of it? Why choose to be unhappy? Spread your wings and fly! Today I am happy, and fulfilled with the goodness of many friends. I continue to enjoy my position as an Academic Counselor. I have *fun*.

25

Grabbing onto the Spool to Finding My Way through a Miracle

I often felt it would take a miracle to rid myself of the emptiness in my entire being. The thread of hope I held onto all my life is what finally led me to search for happiness, maybe for the last time. I hadn't known what that happiness might be, or what it would take for me to be happy, or even know what happiness was. To me, happiness had always been for everyone else. I felt I didn't deserve it; but still, I wanted to earn it.

Pieces of my childhood will forever be imbedded in my mind. The deep hurt that still lingers in my heart from my childhood is bandaged by the forgiveness I later found that now exists deeper in my soul. The pain of losing my brother when I was still young opened my eyes so that I could see how very strong I truly was, but I had to find a way to believe in that strength, I had to find the key to it. I found that there is no such thing as getting *over* losing someone, and that "learning to live with the loss" was a more attainable goal. I learned that I had to love myself before anyone else would.

I've worked my entire life to accept the person I am, always leaving room for growth but trying hard not to be my own worse enemy. I continue to grow daily and appreciate every day and all life has to offer. I am so thankful for all that God has given me. Life is like a garden, with all its beautiful flowers. Among the flowers are weeds, but how I handle what is dealt me is for my choosing. Each experience teaches me about life. I treasure my family, my friends, my health, and most of all my own personal relationship with Jesus Christ, our Lord, my God.

I decided to write this story of my own personal journey in hope that it would help others who are suffering through life and inspire them to never give up. A thread of hope can lead to an endless spool, which lets us know that there is something to grasp onto along the way through harder times. Never give up, because if you do, then you are sure to have nothing, and then what have you proven? Through my darkest days, when the light in my eyes and in my heart was so dim that I could barely see, I hung onto that thread of hope that guided me through my journey, and I am glad I did.

It is said that everything in life has a purpose and that everything happens for a reason. My journey through life has not always been easy and sometimes very difficult to understand. However the experiences in my life have given me strength and a great appreciation for all that life has to offer. Each experience sparked the tenacity that I held deep within my soul. I learned that I was strong enough to prove to myself that I am someone, and I can do whatever I want to do. Most importantly, I gained the gift of believing in myself. My strong desire to help others led me to go all the way and obtain my master's degree in psychological counseling. I not only obtained my degree, but I also went that one step further and received my LMHC (License Mental Health Counselor) designation from the State of Massachusetts. I felt positive and ambitious and knew in my heart that I would not let anything stand in my way. I did it!!!

I am truly happy with my life, I feel complete. I am a woman with a positive, healthy attitude. I counsel and advise students daily as an academic counselor in hopes that I can instill in them what I am so grateful to have achieved in my long journey to finding out who I am. I am "me," and I am thankful everyday for what I have. I have a wonderful, supportive family, many, many, friends, a career that I truly love, and most of all a love of life.

Epilogue
On the Wings of a Dove

I could not finish this book without paying tribute to the person who gave back to me what I almost lost along the way—a life worth living. This is for my therapist, Rick. He will probably chuckle when he reads this chapter, because I remember his modesty when sharing with him my gratitude for all he had done for me. Rick showed me the way back to a life I wanted to live. I remember telling him I was going to write a book, dedicate it to him, and title it "On the Wings of a Dove." I remember him chirping like a bird, teasing me. Perhaps he felt a little embarrassed, but then again maybe not, knowing him as I do.

I had previously seen two other counselors, each for a very short time. The match was not there in either instance. I felt very discouraged. I was ready to feel better. I wanted to feel whole. I was tired of "living on empty." I remember feeling particularly low one day. I was with my sister Debbie, and I expressed to her how I was feeling. She was my angel that day because she gave me the support not to give up, and to keep seeking counseling. She drove me to a clinic where I met with a psychiatrist who evaluated me. He felt that I indeed needed help, and he referred me to a therapist. He informed me that if I wanted a woman counselor the wait would be longer, but if gender didn't matter to me he could refer me to someone almost immediately. This was not a problem for me because I wanted a male counselor. It was very important to me to build up a trust in a male figure.

As promised, almost immediately I had my first appointment with Rick. I knew from the start it was a *match*. During our first session I took the risk to tell him everything that I thought he wouldn't believe or would believe to be exaggerated. I could have cried as I spilled my guts to this stranger. Despite my fears to the contrary, he validated every word I said. It was a miracle in my eyes. He truly believed me! I felt that perhaps a better world was waiting for me, and Rick was going to show me how to find it. I felt he would help me through thick or thin. I had hope, and I finally could have a dream that may come true. Rick gave me that hope. He was part of the woven thread onto which I hung.

Rick eventually opened his own practice in a neighboring town. I had to make the decision whether I would stay with the clinic or move on and continue my therapy with him. My decision came easily to me. I would have gone to China if Rick transferred there. I had finally found someone who believed me; there was no way on earth would I let him go. There was no turning back. I was on a mission. I found myself through Rick. I had never before known who I truly was. I had felt useless and unworthy of anything or anyone, but through Rick's guidance I learned to believe in myself. I learned to love myself.

We traveled to all areas of my world. I knew in my heart that the journey to be well would be long and painful, but I was willing to go to the deepest parts of my mind, heart and soul if it meant freeing myself of the barbed wires that imprisoned me. This is where I wanted to be so I continued therapy until I felt a sense of self worth and I knew who I was. I needed to take control of my life. I knew with the help of my navigator that I could chart my course and find my path. I would eventually find my way to my own paradise island. The keys were in my hand, but I just had to find the right keys to unlock the thick doors of my dark world.

We reached the deepest, darkest areas that blackened my entire being. I discovered that my dreams were attainable. I could finally sing and make beautiful music if I chose to do so. I had sailed magnificently on my journey. I had everything I needed. I had the best therapist/navigator in the world who cared about me and believed in me. I loved him for that, and I love him to this very day for helping me find my way to a life I want to live.

God bless you, Rick!

About the Author

Jacqui DeLorenzo, MS, LMHC, loves being an academic counselor at North Shore Community College, located in Danvers, Massachusetts. A 1979 honor graduate, she has worked more than thirty years serving students with their academic needs, including college adjustments and issues of personal concern. Jacqui's credentials are that she is a licensed mental health counselor in psychological services counseling through the commonwealth of Massachusetts, 1999; and that she received a master of science degree in psychological services/counseling at Salem State College, summa cum laude, in 1997; and a bachelor of science degree in financial aid from the University of Massachusetts, Amherst, summa cum laude, 1987.

Jacqui's first passion is to help students reach their greatest potential. Her goal is to guide each student to a healthy self-esteem that will produce a happy and successful life. She is dedicated to her family and friends, and has a great appreciation for all that life has to offer. She continues to travel whenever she can, and she looks forward to each and every opportunity given to her.

978-0-595-44766-4
0-595-44766-X

Printed in the United States
89062LV00003B/226-234/A

9 780595 447664